RAF Officer & Aircrew Selection Centre (OASC)

www.How2Become.com

Orders: Please contact How2Become Ltd, Suite 1, 60 Churchill Square Business Centre, Kings Hill, Kent ME19 4YU.

You can order through Amazon.co.uk under ISBN 9781907558269, via the website www.How2Become.com, Gardners or Bertrams.

ISBN: 9781907558269

First published 2010

Updated in 2019

Typeset for How2Become Ltd by Anton Pshinka.

Disclaimer

Every effort has been made to ensure that the information contained within this guide is accurate at the time of publication. How2Become Ltd is not responsible for anyone failing any part of any selection process as a result of the information contained within this guide. How2become Ltd and their authors cannot accept any responsibility for any errors or omissions within this guide, however caused. No responsibility for loss or damage occasioned by any person acting, or refraining from action, as a result of the material in this publication can be accepted by How2Become Ltd.

The information within this guide does not represent the views of any third party service or organisation.

CONTENTS

Do you want
to attend a
1-Day
RAF Officer
OASC preparation
training course?

Visit the following website to find out more:

RAFOFFICERCOURSE.CO.UK

Welcome to your new guide – How to pass the RAF Officer selection process. This guide has been designed to help you prepare for, and pass the Royal Air Force Officer selection process, including the Officer and Aircrew Selection Centre.

The author of this guide, Richard McMunn, has spent over 20 years in both the Armed Forces and the Emergency Services. He has vast experience and knowledge in the area of Armed Forces recruitment and you will find his guidance both inspiring and highly informative. During his successful career in the Fire Service, Richard sat on many interview panels assessing candidate's ability to join the Fire Service. He has also been extremely successful at passing job interviews and assessments himself and has a success rate of over 90%. Follow his advice and preparation techniques carefully and you too can achieve the same level of success in your career.

Whilst the selection process for joining the Royal Air Force as an Officer is highly competitive, there are a number of things you can do in order to improve your chances of success, and they are all contained within this guide.

The guide itself has been split up into useful sections to make it easier for you to prepare for each stage. Read each section carefully and take notes as you progress. Don't ever give up on your dreams; if you really want to become an RAF Officer, then you can do it. The way to prepare for a job in the Armed Forces as an Officer is to embark on a programme of 'in-depth' preparation, and this guide will show you exactly how to do just that.

If you need any further help with the RAF Officer aptitude tests, Planning Exercises, getting fit or RAF Officer Interview advice, then we offer a wide range of products to assist you. These are all available through our online shop How2become.com. Once again thank you for your custom and we wish you every success in your pursuit to joining the Royal Air Force.

Work hard, stay focused and be what you want…

Best wishes,

The how2become team

The How2Become Team

Preface by Richard McMunn

I can remember sitting in the Armed Forces careers office in Preston, Lancashire at the age of 16 waiting patiently to see the Warrant Officer who would interview me as part of my application for joining the Royal Navy. I had already passed the written tests, and despite never having sat an interview before in my life, I was confident of success.

In the build up to the interview I had worked very hard studying the job that I was applying for, and also working hard on my interview technique. At the end of the interview I was told that I had easily passed and all that was left to complete was the medical. Unfortunately I was overweight at the time and I was worried that I might fail. At the medical my fears became a reality and I was told by the doctor that I would have to lose a stone in weight before they would accept me. I walked out of the doctor's surgery and began to walk to the bus stop that would take me back home three miles away. I was absolutely gutted, and embarrassed, that I had failed at the final hurdle, all because I was overweight!

I sat at the bus stop feeling sorry for myself and wondering what job I was going to apply for next. My dream of joining the Armed Forces was over and I didn't know which way to turn. Suddenly, I began to feel a sense of determination to lose the weight and get fit in the shortest time possible. It was at that particular point in my life when things would change forever. As the bus approached I remember thinking there was no time like the present for getting started on my fitness regime. I therefore opted to walk the three miles home instead of being lazy and getting the bus. When I got home I sat in my room and wrote out a 'plan of action' that would dictate how I was going to lose the weight required. That plan of action was very simple and it said the following three things:

1. Every weekday morning I will get up at 6am and run 3 miles.

2. Instead of catching the bus to college, and then back home again,
    I will walk.

3. I will eat healthily and I will not go over the recommended daily
    calorific intake.

Every day I would read my simple 'action plan' and it acted as a reminder of what I needed to do. Within a few weeks of following my plan rigidly I had lost over a stone in weight and I was a lot fitter too!

When I returned back to the doctor's surgery for my medical the doctor was amazed that I had managed to lose the weight in such a short space of time and he was pleased that I had been so determined to pass the medical. Six months later I started my basic training course with the Royal Navy.

Ever since then I have always made sure that I prepare properly for any job application. If I do fail a particular interview or section of an application process, then I will always go out of my way to ask for feedback so that I can improve for next time. I also still use an 'action plan' in just about every element of my work today. Action plans allow you to focus your mind on what you want to achieve and I would strongly recommend that you use one during your preparation for the RAF Officer Selection process.

Throughout my career I have always been successful. It's not because I am better than the next person, but simply because I prepare better. I didn't do very well at school so I have to work a lot harder to pass the exams and written tests that form part of a job application process, but I am always aware of what I need to do and what I must improve on.

I have always been a great believer in preparation. Preparation was my key to success, and it will also be yours. Without the right level of preparation you will be setting out on the route to failure. The RAF is hard to join, especially as an Officer, but if you follow the steps that I have compiled within this guide and use them as part of your preparation, then you will increase your chances of success dramatically.

The men and women of the Armed Forces carry out an amazing job. They are there to protect us and our country and they do that job with great pride, passion and very high levels of professionalism and commitment. They are to be congratulated for the job that they do. Before you apply to join the RAF as an Officer you need to be fully confident that you too are capable of providing that same level of commitment. If you think you can do it, and you can rise to the challenge, then you just might be the type of person the RAF is looking for.

Best wishes,

Richard McMunn

Richard McMunn

CHAPTER 1
THE SELECTION PROCESS FOR BECOMING AN RAF OFFICER

The majority of people who will read this guide will have a thorough understanding of what the RAF Officer Selection process consists of. Before I get into each element of selection however, and more importantly how to pass them, it is important for me to briefly explain the different elements.

To begin with, applicants will need to contact their local Armed Forces Careers Office and explain that they wish to apply to become an Officer with the Royal Air Force. The most effective way to do this is to go along to your nearest centre for a brief chat. You will be supplied with an information pack and details on how to apply, providing you meet the minimum eligibility requirements. Alternatively, you can call the careers information line on 0845 605 5555. They will ask for your postcode and then they'll do the rest. You can call from 8am to 8pm Monday to Friday, 9am to 6pm on Saturday, or 10am to 4pm on Sunday.

The Filter Interview

You will eventually be invited to attend what is called a 'filter' interview. This interview is designed to assess whether or not you have the right qualities to become an RAF Officer. If you successfully pass the filter interview, which is usually held at the Armed Forces Careers Office, you will be recommended to attend the Officer and Aircrew Selection Centre (OASC).

The filter interview is, in my opinion, relatively easy to pass. However, you will still need to put in plenty of preparation and I have provided you with a host of sample questions and responses during a later section of this guide.

The Officer and Aircrew Selection Centre

Those applicants who successfully pass the filter interview and preliminary checks will need to attend the Officers and Aircrew Selection Centre (OASC) which takes place at the RAF College Cranwell in Lincolnshire. The Royal Air Force has been assessing candidates for Officer Selection at Cranwell for many years now. In total there are approximately 95 'boards' every year. 2400 candidates will go through selection, with approximately 500 places being offered. That effectively means that only 1 out of 5 people who attend the OASC are successful.

The important thing to remember is that you are going to be the successful one out of the five, as opposed to one of the unsuccessful four. How do you achieve this?

Simple, you understand the selection process and the scoring criteria, and then you go all out to prepare fully for every different element of the OASC.

Whilst at the OASC you will undergo a series of tests and assessments as follows:

Part 1 OASC

The first part of OASC is a series of aptitude tests. The career you're interested in will determine what tests you need to pass before you can join. These Computer Based Aptitude Tests (CBAT) will only be taken if the job position you are applying for requires it. For example, in order to become a pilot you will be required to undergo a series of extended tests.

The aptitude tests are designed to assess your ability to carry out certain tasks, such as:

- how well you respond physically to visual information;
- your ability to interpret information in two dimensions and devise a three-dimensional solution;
- your ability to complete several tasks simultaneously;
- deductive reasoning;
- spatial reasoning;
- work rate and concentration;
- verbal and numerical reasoning.

Candidates must pass the CBAT if they wish to continue on with the rest of the OASC.

Part 2 OASC

Part 2 of the OASC comprises of the following assessments:

- Group discussion;
- Group planning exercise;
- Hangar familiarisation;
- Leaderless task;
- Command situation task;
- Interview;
- Selection fitness test.

All of the exercises, with the exception of the Individual Problem exercise, will require candidates to work in syndicates of five or six.

The Discussion exercise entails a group discussion about different topics which are normally provided by the Board. The Group Planning exercise and the Individual Problem exercise involve a theoretical problem featuring time and distance calculations. As the names suggests the syndicate must work as a team in the Group Planning exercise while in the Individual Problem exercise each candidate works and is tested alone.

Both the Leaderless exercise and the Command Situation exercise involve the solution of a 'practical' problem over an 'obstacle course'. In the Leaderless exercise there is no 'appointed' leader whereas in the Command Situation exercise each candidate takes a turn as leader and must direct the rest of the syndicate.

The assessments during the selection centre are carried out by 'Selection Boards'. Each Board consists of a Board Chairman and a Board Member, and is presided over by a more experienced Board President. The President oversees no more than two Boards simultaneously and his final decision takes precedence over that of the Board.

In general, the aptitude testing and elements of the medical examination assess particular requirements for specific branch specialisations, such as pilot and navigator, whereas the Part 1 interview and the Part 2 exercises assess candidates' personal qualities (PQs), i.e. their potential for Initial Officer Training (IOT) or the NCA Initial Training Course. The IOT and the NCA Initial Training courses are the first stages in an officer's career in the RAF and include fitness development, military training and academic study as well as practical outdoor leadership challenges.

The competencies required to demonstrate leadership potential as an RAF Officer are interpersonal, problem solving and character competencies. These will be explained in the next two sections of this guide.

The Qualities Required to Become an RAF Officer

Many candidates who attend OASC will be under prepared. In addition to this, many candidates will spend hours scouring internet chat forums in an attempt to find hints and tips on how to pass OASC. Whilst there is nothing wrong with this, the most effectively prepared candidates are those who concentrate primarily on demonstrating the key assessable qualities in order to become an RAF Officer.

The whole purpose of the OASC is to determine whether or not you have the 'potential' to become an RAF Officer. If you have the potential, then there is a greater chance that you will pass Initial Officer Training. The RAF will be investing literally hundreds of thousands of pounds into your development and career progression. Therefore, they want to be sure that you have the potential to pass every stage of training.

In order to assess the potential, the RAF will assess you against a series of qualities and competencies. Before I move on to the scoring criteria I want to talk a little about the qualities that you need to demonstrate during the entire selection process. You will notice that after each list of qualities I have provided you with some useful tips.

Qualities That You Need to Demonstrate

- Determined
- Resolute
- Persistent
- Unwavering

- Steady
- Able to overcome most difficulties
- Strong-willed.

You are applying to join the RAF as an Officer. Therefore, it is crucial that you are able to remain calm in a crisis, be totally focused on achieving the end result and be determined to succeed at everything you do.

For example, during the planning exercise stage you will be placed under considerable pressure by the assessing Officers. If you do not know the answer to a question, then it is better to say so, rather than panic, waffle or crumble under the pressure. One of the main purposes of OASC is to determine whether or not you have the ability to stay focused under pressure.

- Imaginative
- Initiative
- Constructive
- Perceptive
- Original
- Mentally agile

- Inventive
- Visionary
- Intelligent
- Mature
- Balanced.

These qualities are predominantly focused on your state of mind. Do you have the ability to come up with solutions to problems? Can you think outside the box? Can you see the end result? Are you sensible and mature for your years? During every stage of OASC make sure you remain level-headed. Do not act in a foolhardy way and always think before you speak. Engage your brain before you engage your mouth!

- Forceful
- Compelling
- Persuasive
- Powerful
- Vigorous
- Assertive
- Consistent

- Effective
- Resourceful
- Magnetic
- Inspiring
- Considerate
- Considerable impact.

Let us assume that you are participating in the Group Planning Exercise phase. You have worked hard during your preparation in the build up to OASC and you are very confident that your plan of tackling the exercise is the most effective. However, two other members of your group have alternative solutions to the problem. What do you do? The options are simple – you can either go along with their desired solutions(s) or you can have the confidence in your own abilities and your plan and attempt to 'persuade' them both that your option is the most effective. If I was attending OASC, I would have the confidence in my own abilities and persuade them that my option is the most effective.

Remember – you are applying to become an RAF Officer and that means you are applying to become a leader!

- Bold
- Daring
- Courageous
- Entrepreneurial
- Enthusiastic
- Spirit of adventure
- Untiring
- Energetic

- Active
- Diligent
- Industrious
- Persevering
- Physically strong and active
- Organiser
- Sense of urgency.

During the indoor and outdoor tasks, be sure to get involved. Those people who believe if they sit on the fence and don't get involved, they will go unnoticed, are sorely mistaken. You must get involved, come up with solutions, encourage the team, support others and try your hardest to achieve every task that you are set.

- Tolerant
- Flexible
- Co-operative
- Diplomatic

- Tactful
- Resilient (never gives in)
- Adaptable
- Willing to accept responsibility.

What are you like towards other people? Do you have the ability to work with others as part of a team? Every team encounters problems along the way. How you deal with those problems is what matters. Be tolerant of other people, always be flexible in your approach to tasks, never give in and be the first to put your hand up when they ask for a volunteer.

- Sensible
- Respective
- Shrewd
- Well-balanced
- Decisive

- Discerning
- Fair
- Unbiased
- Loyal
- Steadfast.

I have now provided you with plenty of qualities that all go towards making an effective RAF Officer. So, when the interview panel asks you the question "What are the qualities of an RAF Officer?" you will have no problem answering it!

You are a Leader and a Manager

RAF Officers are both leaders and managers. Therefore, it is important that you understand the difference between each of them and how they are interlinked.

In order to become a competent RAF Officer you will need to be effective at both. Here's a brief explanation of how they differ:

Leader – A leader is someone who effectively takes a team of people from point A to point B. These two 'points' don't have to be in terms of distance, but instead they could be a mission or a company or organisational goal. For example, it might be a football manager attempting to lead his or her team to promotion to a higher league. A leader should be a visionary. They should 'see' where they want their team to be and take steps to get them there.

Manager – A manager is someone who arranges and uses resources in order to achieve a company's or organisation's goal. Examples of resources are:

• People;
• Utilities such as water, gas and electricity;
• Vehicles and equipment;
• Paper and pencils;
• Fuel;
• Time.

An effective manager will use his or her resources effectively. They will not waste resources and they will use them appropriately. A manager's greatest asset is his/her people whom which they command. When you join the RAF as an Officer you will undoubtedly be responsible at some point in your career for a group or team of people. How you manage them is very important.

How Do They Work Together?

During my time in the Fire Service I served as an Officer for many years. Without wishing to blow my own trumpet, I was a highly effective manager and leader. Managerial and leadership skills are interlinked and you will draw on each of these assets at different times during your career as an RAF Officer. For example, whilst attending severe fires and road traffic collisions in the Fire Service, I was required to use both leadership and managerial skills at the same time in order to achieve the required task. I would always have a plan that was discussed with my Junior Officers. I would assign people and equipment (resources) to carry out certain tasks at the incident. I would order equipment, fuel and refreshments (resources) well in advance of them running out. I would arrange many hours in advance for relief crews to attend the incident in order to replace my tiring firefighters. I would support my team and I would communicate effectively with them during every stage of the incident. At the end of the incident I would always hold an incident debrief. This would allow me to thank everyone for their efforts and allow us to identify any areas of improvement for future incidents.

All of these actions were using my 'managerial' skills. In terms of leadership skills, I would brief my team well in order to explain the plan and what it was that needed to be done. I would provide words of support and encouragement throughout the operation and I would listen carefully to my junior officer's advice and suggestions during every stage of the incident.

Being an officer in the Royal Air Force is about drawing on different skills and assets in order to achieve a task or goal. That goal may take many years to achieve and may not necessarily be a short term objective. Always remember that in order to become a competent RAF Officer, you will need to be an effective leader and manager.

CHAPTER 2
THE RAF OFFICER
FILTER INTERVIEW

During the RAF Officer Selection process you will be required to sit a number of interviews, both at the Armed Forces Careers Office and also at the Officer and Aircrew Selection Centre (OASC). The first interview will be held at your local Armed Forces Careers Office and will be undertaken with a member of the RAF recruitment team. This interview is more commonly referred to as the 'filter' interview and its purpose is, as the name suggests, to filter out those people who have a good chance of passing OASC and those who do not.

The duration of the interview will very much depend on your responses to the questions. However, you can expect the interview to last for approximately 30 minutes. The questions that you will be assessed against during the initial interview will normally be taken from the following areas:

- The reasons why you want to join the RAF;
- The reasons why you want to become an Officer;
- What choice of career/branch you are most interested in, the reason for choosing that career/branch, and the skills you have to match the role;
- What information you already know about the RAF, its lifestyle and training;
- Information relating to your hobbies and interests including sporting/team activities;
- Any personal responsibilities that you currently have at home, in your education or at work;
- Information about your family and your partner and what they think about you joining;
- Information based around your initial application;
- Your experience of work and education;
- Your managerial and leadership experiences to date;
- Your emotional stability and your maturity;
- Your drive and determination to succeed;
- Having a positive reaction to a disciplined environment and towards people in positions of authority.

Before I move on to a number of sample interview questions and responses I want to explain a little bit about interview techniques and how you can come across in a positive manner during the interview. During my career in the Fire Service I sat on many interview panels assessing people who wanted to become firefighters. As you can imagine there were some good applicants and there were also some poor ones. Let me explain the difference between a good applicant and a poor one.

A Good Applicant

A good applicant is someone who has taken the time to prepare. They have researched both the organisation they are applying to join and also the role that they are being interviewed for. They may not know every detail about the organisation and the role, but it will be clear that they have made an effort to find out important facts and information. They will be well presented at the interview and they will be confident, but not over confident. As soon as they walk into the interview room they will be polite and courteous and they will sit down in the interview chair only when invited to do so. Throughout the interview they will sit up right in the chair and communicate in a positive manner. If they do not know the answer to a question, they will say so and they won't try and waffle. At the end of the interview they will ask positive questions about the job or the organisation before shaking hands and leaving.

A Poor Applicant

A poor applicant could be any combination of the following. They will be late for the interview or even forget to turn up at all. They will have made little effort to dress smart and they will have carried out little or no preparation. When asked questions about the job or the organisation they will have little or no knowledge. Throughout the interview they will appear to be unenthusiastic about the whole process and will look as if they want the interview to be over as soon as possible. Whilst sat in the interview chair they will slouch and fidget. At the end of the interview they will try to ask clever questions that are intended to impress the panel.

I strongly advise that you try out a mock interview before you attend the filter interview. You'll be amazed at how much your confidence will improve. All you need to do is get your parents or a friend to sit down with you and ask you the interview questions that are contained within this guide. Try to answer them as if you were at the real interview. The more mock interviews you try, the more confident you'll become.

Now let's take a look at a number of sample interview questions. Please note that these questions are not guaranteed to be the exact ones you'll come up against at the real filter interview, but they are a great starting point in your preparation. Use the sample responses that I have provided as a basis for your own preparation. Construct your answers on your own opinions and experiences.

Sample Interview Question Number 1

"Why do you want to join the Royal Air Force?"

This is an almost guaranteed question during the filter interview so there should be no reason why you can't answer it in a positive manner. Only you will know the real reason why you want to join but consider the following benefits before you construct your response:

- A career in the RAF presents a challenge that is not available in the majority of other jobs or careers;
- A career in the RAF will provide you with professional training and on-going personal development;
- A career in the RAF will offer you the chance to work in a highly professional organisation that prides itself on high standards;
- The RAF is an organisation that people have a huge amount of respect for. Therefore those people who join it are very proud to be a part of such a team.

Try to display a good level of motivation when answering questions of this nature. The Royal Air Force is looking for people who want to become a professional member of their team and who understand their way of life. It should be your own decision to join the Royal Air Force and you should be attracted to what this career has to offer. If you have been pushed into joining by your family, then you shouldn't be there! There now follows a sample response to this question.

Sample Response to Interview Question Number 1

"Why do you want to join the Royal Air Force?"

'I have wanted to join the Royal Air Force for a couple of years now and I have been working very hard to pass selection. Having studied the RAF recruitment literature and the RAF website I am impressed by the professionalism and standards the service sets itself. I would like a career that is fulfilling, challenging and rewarding and I believe that the RAF would provide all of these. During my research I have spoken to serving members of the RAF and every single one of them has had positive things to say about the service.

Over the last few years I have become more aware of my own skills and qualities and I believe these would be very well suited to the RAF and in particular the role of an Officer. I enjoy being away from home and I also like to take responsibility. For example, I was recently made captain of my football team and this involves organising team trips and fixtures. I am also a good team player and I like working with different groups of people who have different experiences in life. There is always something to learn in life and I would love to be a part of a service such as the RAF where I would be continually learning new skills.

I have seriously considered the implications that joining a service such as the RAF would have on both my personal life and social life and I have discussed these with my family and my partner. They have given me their full support and they promise to help me achieve my goal of joining the Royal Air Force. Even though I know the Initial Officer Training will be hard, I am certain I can pass it with flying colours and if I am successful at this interview and the OASC, I promise that I will work very hard to pass every exam.'

Sample Interview Question Number 2

"What does your family think of you wanting to join the Royal Air Force?"

What your family think about you wanting to join the RAF is very important, simply for the reason that you will need their support both during your training and during your career. I can remember my parents being fully behind my decision to join the Armed Forces and I'm glad that they were for a very good reason. After about two weeks into my basic training I started to feel a little bit home sick; like any young man would do being away from home for a long period of time. I rang my father and discussed with him how I felt. After talking to him on the phone, I felt perfectly fine and I no longer felt homesick. During that conversation he reminded me how hard I had worked to get a place on the course and that he and my mother wanted me to succeed. For that reason alone I was glad that I had the support of my parents.

Before you apply to join the RAF it is important that you discuss your choice of career with either your parents or your guardian. If you have a partner, then obviously you will need to discuss this with them too. If they have any concerns whatsoever, then I would advise you take them along with you to the Armed Forces Careers Office so they can discuss these concerns with the trained recruitment staff. Get their full support as you may need it at some point during your career, just like I did.

There now follows a sample response to this question to help you prepare.

Sample Response to Interview Question Number 2

"What does your family think of you wanting to join the Royal Air Force?"

'Before I made my application I discussed my choice of career with both my parents and my partner. Initially they were apprehensive but they could see how motivated and excited I was as I explained everything I had learnt so far about the service. I showed them the recruitment literature and even took them around an RAF museum to get them on board with my application. I understand that it is important they support me during my application and I now have their full backing. In fact, they are now more excited about the fact I'll be leaving home than I am! I have also told them everything I know about the training I will go through and the conditions I will serve under. They are aware that the Royal Air Force has a brilliant reputation and this has helped them to further understand why I want to join. They are also looking forward to hopefully seeing me at my passing out parade if I am successful and therefore I have their full backing.'

Sample Interview Question Number 3

"What responsibilities do you have either at work, school or at home?"

When you join the RAF you will automatically become responsible for a number of things. As an Officer there will be a higher level of expectation and your duties/ responsibilities will naturally increase. Apart from being responsible for the upkeep of your kit and your equipment, you will also have additional responsibilities such as cleaning, ironing and making sure you are on time for every lesson, tutorial and drill. Those people who have had little or no experience whatsoever prior to joining may find this new burden difficult to cope with. Therefore, having already held positions of responsibility prior to applying as an Officer will work in your favour. If you've never had any responsibility in your life, then now is the time to make a change. Start taking responsibility for household tasks such as the washing and cleaning. Learn how to iron your own clothes or take on a part time/full time job that requires you to be responsible for a specific role. It will certainly be an advantage if you also have some form of managerial or leadership skills.

You may decide to join a group or youth organisation such as the air cadets or scouts. Whatever you do, make sure you are responsible for carrying out set tasks and jobs and also make sure you carry out those jobs professionally and to the best of your ability.

Now take a look at the following sample response to this question.

Sample Response to Interview Question Number 3

"What responsibilities do you have either at work, school or at home?"

'I currently hold a few responsibilities both at home and in my part time job. I'm responsible for cleaning the house top to bottom once a week and I usually do this on a Sunday before I go and play football for my local team. I'm also captain of my football team which means I have to arrange the fixtures, book the football ground and I also collect the kit at the end of the match and get it washed and dried for the following week's fixture.

I have just started a new job at my local supermarket where I'm responsible for serving customers and making sure stock levels are kept up. This involves cross checking current stock levels with required standards and I have to report daily to my manager with any discrepancies or missing items or goods. Whilst serving the customer I'm responsible for ensuring I give them a good level of service and I also have to check people for identification if they appear to be under the required age to purchase alcohol or cigarettes.

More recently I took on a temporary supervisor's role at work. The vacancy had arisen and I was first in the queue to apply for the job. I now have a number of people whom report directly to me. I make sure that I take this additional responsibility very seriously. I enjoy taking on responsibility as it gives me a sense of achievement. I understand that I will need to be responsible during my Initial RAF Officer Training for not only the upkeep of my kit and equipment, but I'll also have to make sure I am punctual and that I make the time to study hard in the evening for my exams.'

Sample Interview Question Number 4

"How do you think you will cope with the discipline, regimentation and the additional responsibilities that come with being an Officer in the Royal Air Force?"

When you join the RAF you will be joining a military organisation that has set procedures, standards and discipline codes, and these are there for a very good reason. They ensure that the organisation operates at its optimum best and without these much could go wrong, and people could either be injured or at worst, killed. To some people these important aspects of RAF life will come as a shock when they join. The RAF recruitment staff will want to know that you are fully prepared for this change in lifestyle. They are investing time, effort and resources into your training so they want to know that you can cope with their way of life.

When answering this type of question you need to demonstrate both your awareness of what the RAF life involves and also your positive attitude towards the disciplined environment. Study the recruitment literature and visit the careers website to get a feel for the type of training you will be going through. I have now provided you with a sample response to this question.

Sample Response to Interview Question Number 4

"How do you think you will cope with the discipline, regimentation and the additional responsibilities that come with being an Officer in the Royal Air Force?"

'I believe I would cope with it very well. In the build up to selection I have been trying to implement routine and discipline into my daily life. I've been getting up at 6am every weekday morning and going on a 3 mile run. This will hopefully prepare me for the early starts that I'll encounter during Initial Officer Training. I've also been learning how to iron my own clothes and I've been helping around the house with the cleaning and washing, much to the surprise of my parents!

I fully understand that the RAF needs a disciplined workforce if it is to function as effectively as it does. Without that discipline things could go wrong and if I did not carry out my duties professionally, then I could endanger somebody's life. As an Officer in the RAF it is even more important that you are capable of following rules, policies and procedures. After all, we are all working towards achieving the defence mission and the mission/vision of the RAF.

I fully understand why discipline is required and believe I would cope with it well. I understand that being in the RAF isn't a 9-5 job but instead you are required to take on tasks whenever required. I have read all of the RAF recruitment literature and I know there are people from every background working in the team. I know that I can bring something to the team too.'

Sample Interview Question Number 5

"How do you think you will cope with being away from home and losing your personal freedom?"

This type of question is one that needs to be answered positively. The most effective way to respond to it is to provide the recruitment staff with examples of where you have already lived away from home for a period of time. This could be either with your school or college, an adventure trip, camping with friends or even with a youth organisation. Try to think of occasions when you have had to fend for yourself or even 'rough it' during camps or adventure trips. If you are already an active person who spends very little time sat at home in front of the television or computer, then you will probably have no problem with losing your personal freedom. During your time in the RAF there'll be very little time to sit around doing nothing anyway. So, if you're used to being active before you join, then this is a plus.

Take a look at the sample response that now follows and try to structure your own response around this.

Sample Response to Interview Question Number 5

"How do you think you will cope with being away from home and losing your personal freedom?"

'I already have some experience of being away from home so I believe I would cope quite well. Whilst serving with the Air Cadets I was introduced to the RAF way of life and I fully understand what it is like to be away from home. Having said that, I am not complacent and I have been working hard to improve my fitness and academic skills. To be honest with you, I'm not the kind of person who sits around at home watching television or sitting at the computer, so I'm hardly indoors anyway. In terms of losing my personal freedom I'm looking forward to the routine and regimentation that the RAF will provide as I believe this will bring some positive structure to my life. Even though I am young I want to ensure that I have a good future and I believe a career in the RAF will bring me just that, providing that is, I work hard during training.

During my time in the Air Cadets I've been away on a couple of camps and I really enjoyed this. We learnt how to fend for ourselves whilst away and I loved the fact that I was meeting new and interesting people. I understand that RAF training will be difficult and intense but I am fully prepared for this. I am confident that I will cope with the change in lifestyle very well.'

Sample Interview Question Number 6

"Are you involved in any sporting activities and how do you keep yourself fit?"

This is an almost guaranteed question during the RAF filter interview so make sure you have something positive to respond with. When answering questions based around your own physical fitness and the types of sporting activities you are involved in you need to be honest, but bear in mind the following points:

Although you don't have to be super fit to join the RAF you do need to have a good level of physical fitness, so being fit in the first instance is obviously an advantage. The RAF prides themselves on their ability to work as an effective team unit. Those people who engage in active team sports are more likely to be competent team members and good leaders of men and women. If you play a team sport, then this will be a good thing to tell the interviewers. If you don't, then it might be a good idea to go and join one!

Regardless of the above points, remember that if you don't do any physical activity whatsoever, then you will score low in this area. Make sure you partake in some form of physical activity. You should also bear in mind that you will be required to pass the bleep test during your time at the OASC.

There now follows a sample response to help you prepare.

Sample Response to Interview Question Number 6

"Are you involved in any sporting activities and how do you keep yourself fit?"

'Yes I am. I currently play in my local netball team and have been doing so for a number of years now. Maintaining a good level of fitness is something I enjoy. In fact, in addition to my netball involvement I also go running 3 times a week. I'm aware that during the initial RAF Officer training course I will be pushed to my limits so I need to be prepared for that. I believe the fact that I play team sports will help me get through my training.

I enjoy playing in the netball team because when we are losing to another team everyone always pulls together and we work hard to try and win the game back. After the game we all meet in the club bar for a drink and chat about the game. At the next training session we always work on our weak areas and try to look for ways to improve as a team. Keeping fit is important to me and something that I want to continue throughout my career if I am successful in joining the RAF. I have also been working hard to pass the pre-joining fitness test and I have made sure that I can easily pass the minimum standard'.

Sample Interview Question Number 7

"What do you think the qualities of a good team player are?"

As you are already aware, the RAF prides itself on the ability to operate as an effective team member. Therefore, having knowledge of how a team operates and the qualities required to become a competent team player would be an advantage. Whilst you will be required to lead teams as an Officer, you will still be required to perform effectively as a team member.

Let us take a quick look at some of the qualities required in order to become an effective team member:

- An ability to interact and work with others, regardless of their age, sex, religion, sexual orientation, background, disability or appearance;
- Being able to communicate with everyone in the team and provide the appropriate level of support and encouragement;
- Being capable of carrying out tasks correctly, professionally and in accordance with guidelines and regulations;
- Being focused on the team's goal(s);
- Having a flexible attitude and approach to the task;
- Putting the needs of the team first before your own;
- Putting personal differences aside for the sake of the team;
- Being able to listen to others suggestions and contributions.

When responding to this type of question it would be an advantage if you could back up your response with an example of where you already work in a team. Take a look at the following sample response before creating your own based on your own experiences and ideas.

Sample Response to Interview Question Number 7

"What do you think the qualities of a good team player are?"

'A good team player must have many different qualities including an ability to listen carefully to a given brief. If you don't listen to the brief that is provided, then you can't complete the task properly. In addition to listening carefully to the brief you must be able to communicate effectively with everyone in the team. This will include providing support for the other team members and also listening to other people's suggestions on how a task can be achieved. You also have to be able to work with anyone in the team regardless of their age, background, religion, sexual orientation, disability or appearance. You can't discriminate against anyone and if you do, then there is no place for you within that team. A good team player must also be able to carry out his or her job professionally and competently. When I say competently I mean correctly and in accordance with guidelines and training. You should also be focused on the team's goal and not be distracted by any external factors. Putting the needs of the team first is paramount. Finally a good team player must be flexible and be able to adapt to the changing requirements of the team.

I already have some experience of working in a team and I know how important it is to work hard at achieving the task. I have a part time job at weekends working in my local supermarket and every week we have a team briefing. During the team briefings my manager will inform us what jobs need to be carried out as a priority. During one particular meeting he asked three of us to clear a fire escape that had become blocked with cardboard boxes, debris and rubbish. He also asked us to come up with a plan to prevent it from happening again. We quickly set about the task carefully removing the rubbish and I had the responsibility of arranging for a refuse collection company to come and dispose of the rubbish. We also had to work together to find ways of preventing the rubbish from being haphazardly disposed in the same way again in the future. We sat down together and wrote out a memorandum for our manager that he could distribute to all staff. At the end of the job we'd worked well to achieve the task and no more rubbish was ever disposed in the fire escape again. My manager was very pleased with the job we'd done.'

Sample Interview Question Number 8

"What do you do in your spare time?"

With questions of this nature the Royal Air Force recruitment staff are looking to see if you use your leisure time wisely. This will tell them a lot about your attitude and motivation. We all know that some people spend their spare time doing nothing, or watching TV and playing computer games. When you join the RAF you won't have much time do nothing, so tell them that you are active and that you are doing worthwhile things. For example, if you are involved in any sports, outdoor activities or are part of any youth organisation such as the Air Cadets, then these are good things to tell them. You may also be involved in voluntary work or charity work and, once again, such pastimes will work in your favour if mentioned at interview. If you currently do very little with your spare time, then now is a good time to make a lifestyle change. Embark on a fitness routine or join an activity club or organisation.

Sample Response to Interview Question Number 8

"What do you do in your spare time?"

'During my spare time I like to keep active, both physically and mentally. I enjoy visiting the gym three times a week and I have a structured workout that I try and vary every few months to keep my interest up. When I attend the gym I like to work out using light weights and I also enjoy using the indoor rower. I always try and beat my best time over a 2000 metre distance.

I'm also currently doing a weekly evening class in Judo, which is one of my hobbies. I haven't achieved any grades yet but I am taking my first one in a few weeks time. I'm also a member of the local Air Cadet Force, which is an evening's commitment every week and the occasional weekend. Of course, I know when it is time to relax and usually do this by either listening to music or playing snooker with my friends but, overall, I'm quite an active person. I certainly don't like sitting around doing nothing. I understand that if I'm successful in joining the RAF there will be plenty of things to do in the evenings to keep me occupied, such as the free gym and other various social events.'

Sample Interview Question Number 9

"Can you tell me about any achievements you have experienced during your life so far?"

Those people who can demonstrate a history of achievement during the RAF interview are far more likely to pass the Initial Officer Training course. Demonstrating a history of achievement already will work in your favour. Having achieved something in your life demonstrates that you have the ability to see things through to the end, something which is crucial to your career in the RAF as an Officer. It also shows that you are motivated and determined to succeed.

Try to think of examples where you have succeeded or achieved something relevant in your life. Some good examples of achievements are as follows:

• Winning a trophy with a football or hockey team;
• Taking on responsibility at work, school or university;
• GCSE's, A Levels, Degrees and other educational qualifications;
• Duke of Edinburgh's Awards;
• Raising money for charity.

Obviously you will have your own achievements that you want to add in your response, but take a look at the following sample response to this question.

Once you have read it try to think of occasions in your life where you have achieved something of importance.

Sample Response to Interview Question Number 9

"Can you tell me about any achievements you have experienced during your life so far?"

'Yes I can. So far in my life I have achieved quite a few things that I am proud of. To begin with I achieved good grades whilst at school including a grade 'A' in English and Mathematics. I then went on to achieve good A level results before finally completing my degree last year. I worked very hard to achieve my grades and I'm proud of them. At weekends I play rugby for a local team and I've achieved a number of things with them. Apart from winning the league last year we also held a charity match against the local Police rugby team. We managed to raise £500 for a local charity which was a great achievement.

More recently I managed to achieve a huge increase in my fitness levels. Because I am applying to join the RAF as an Officer I have been working very hard to improve my strength, fitness and overall stamina. I have increased my scores on the bleep test and I can now swim fifty lengths of my local pool. When I started I could hardly mange ten lengths! I have learnt that you have to work hard in life if you want to achieve things and I have a good positive attitude to hard work. My own personal motto is 'work hard and you'll be rewarded'.

Sample Interview Question Number 10

"What are your strengths and what are you good at?"

This is a common interview question that is relatively easy to answer. The problem with it is that many people use the same response. It is quite an easy thing to tell the interviewer that you are dedicated and the right person for the job. However, it is a different thing backing it up with evidence!

If you are asked this type of question, make sure you are positive during your response and show that you actually mean what you are saying. Then, back up the strengths you have mentioned with examples of when you have shown something that you say you are. For example, if you tell the panel that you are a motivated person, back it up with an example in your life where you have achieved something through sheer motivation and determination.

Sample Response to Interview Question Number 10

"What are your strengths and what are you good at?"

'To begin with, I'm a determined person who likes to see things through to the end. For example, I recently ran a marathon for charity. I'd never done this kind of thing before and found it very hard work, but I made sure I completed the task. Another strength of mine is that I'm always looking for ways to improve myself. As an example, I have been preparing for the RAF selection process by performing mock mathematical tests.

I noticed that I was getting a number of fraction and decimal questions wrong, so in order to improve I decided to get some personal tuition at my college to ensure that I could pass this part of the test. Finally, I would say that one of my biggest strengths is that I'm a great team player. I really enjoy working in a team environment and achieving things through a collaborative approach. For example, I play in a local rugby team and we recently won the league trophy for the first time since the club was established some 50 years ago.'

Sample Interview Question Number 11

"What are your weaknesses?"

Now this is a difficult question to answer. We all have weaknesses and anyone who says they haven't, is probably not telling the truth. However, you must be very careful how you respond to this question. Apart from being truthful you must also provide a weakness that you are working hard on to improve. You should also remember that you are joining a disciplined service that requires hard work, determination and a will to succeed. So, if you are the type of person who cannot get up in the morning, keeps making regular mistakes and is averse to responsibility, then the RAF is definitely not for you.

The key to responding to this type of question is to be truthful but to also back it up with examples of what you are doing to improve your weakness. Take a look at the following example.

Sample Response to Interview Question Number 11

"What are your weaknesses?"

'I have to be honest, whilst studying for the RAF aptitude tests I found that I wasn't particularly good at the numerical reasoning questions. Even though I did achieve excellent GCSE and A Level grades at school, I seemed to be struggling with these questions. Despite this, I didn't let this deter me in my pursuit to joining the RAF as an Officer so I decided to get some personal tuition at my local college. I managed to find a free evening class that helped me to understand how to carry out the questions. After a couple of week's tuition I soon noticed a big improvement in my scores and my ability to answer these questions. I'm still attending the evening classes which I've found to be a great boost to my confidence. I feel very confident that when I do come to sit the tests I'll be able to achieve the required scores.'

Sample Interview Question Number 12

"Can you tell me what you have learnt about your chosen career?"

Once again, an almost guaranteed question, so make sure you prepare for it fully. The only information you will need is either in the recruitment literature that you're provided with, or on the RAF careers website at www.raf.mod.uk. For example, if you want to join the RAF as a Logistics Officer, then visit the website and read up on the information available regarding this career. I also advise that you learn as much as possible about the training that you'll be required to undertake if you are successful. You should also ask your AFCO recruitment advisor for more information relating to your chosen career and training. They will be able to point you in the right direction.

Sample Interview Question Number 13

"What has attracted you to your chosen career?"

This type of question is designed to see if there are any genuine reasons why you have chosen your particular career. Some applicants get carried away with the glamour of some of the posts that are available; without putting any serious thought into why they actually want the job. When preparing your response to this question you need to think about the skills you have already gained that are relevant to the role, and also any experiences you have that would assist you in becoming competent at that role.

Previous experiences and skills are not a pre-requisite for some jobs in the RAF; however, you will need to provide genuine reasons why you have chosen your particular choice of career.

Sample Interview Question Number 14

"Can you tell me whereabouts in the world the RAF are operating right now?"

If you put plenty of work into your preparation, then you will undoubtedly get to find out the whereabouts of the RAF around the world. Of course, this will change as the weeks and month's progress but one of the most effective ways to find out where the RAF are operating right now is to visit the Ministry of Defence website at www. mod.uk. From here you will be able to access instant and up to date information relevant to the RAF's current operations. Remember to regularly check the website for updates.

Sample Interview Question Number 15

"What are the different ranks for both non-commissioned and commissioned staff in the RAF?"

This question assesses your knowledge of the ranks within the RAF. It is a simple question and one that should be relatively easy to respond to. Having an understanding of the different ranks for both commissioned and non-commissioned staff will be an obvious advantage for when you start your Initial Officer Training. Basically, as you are probably aware, 'commissioned' staff are Officers within the RAF. The 'commission' is earnt following the successful completion of training and it is received from the Queen. The commission entitles an Officer in the RAF to give orders to other people who are at a lower rank than themselves.

Here are the ranks within the RAF for you to study. You may also decide to study the different markings for each rank prior to your interview.

Non-commissioned staff

▼

Leading Aircraftman/Aircraftwoman

▼

SAC Technician

▼

Senior Aircraftman/Aircraftwoman (SAC)

▼

Junior Technician

▼

Corporal

▼

Sergeant

▼

Chief Technician

▼

Flight Sergeant

▼

Warrant Officer

Commissioned staff

Pilot Officer

Flying Officer

Flight Lieutenant

Squadron Leader

Wing Commander

Group Captain

Air Commodore

Sample Interview Question Number 16

"Name five different RAF bases and their roles."

There are many different RAF bases around the UK and also around the world. Learning all of their names and their roles would be quite a task. However, I believe it is important that you at least know the names, locations and the roles of a number of them. On the RAF website you will be able to find details about each individual airbase and the roles each one carried out.

Take a look at the following sample response to this question.

Sample Response to Interview Question Number 16

"Name five different RAF bases and their roles."

'During my research I studied the many different airbases and I even managed to visit a couple of them. The first airbase that I studied is RAF Brize Norton which is based in Caterton, Oxfordshire. This airbase is the largest in the UK and from here the RAF operate air transportation services and air-to-air refuelling operations. In addition to holding large numbers of aircraft such as the VC10 and the TriStar K1 it is also the home of the Parachute Training School. Then there is RAF Gibraltar which is manned by RAF staff. There are no aircraft based there but the airbase is still used by many visiting aircraft. Although I never visited RAF Gibraltar I am aware of its significance as an RAF base. RAF Honnington is located at Bury St Edmunds, Suffolk and this is the RAF Regiment depot. Aircrafts have not been at this base since 1993. RAF Uxbridge is based in Middlesex and this is the home of the Number 63 RAF Regiment Squadron and is also the HQ for Music Services. Finally I studied RAF Odiham which is located in Hampshire. Based at RAF Odiham are a number of different Chinook Helicopter Squadrons such as number 7 Squadron, number 18 Squadron and number 27 Squadron.'

Final Interview Tips

Within this section of the guide I will provide you with some final tips that will help you prepare for the RAF filter interview. Remember that your success will very much depend on how prepared you are. Don't forget to work on your interview technique, carry out plenty of research and work on your responses to the interview questions.

- In the build up to the interview carry out plenty of targeted preparation work. Read your recruitment literature and spend time studying the RAF website. Ask the AFCO recruitment advisor to provide you with information about the training you'll undergo for both your chosen career and also your Initial Officer Training;

- Work on your interview technique and make sure you try out at least one mock interview. This involves getting your family or friends to sit you down and ask you the interview questions that are contained within this guide;

- When you receive your date for the filter interview make sure you turn up on time. Check your travel and parking arrangements the day before your interview. The last thing you need is to be late for your interview!

- Think carefully about what you are going to wear during the interview. I am not saying that you should go out and buy an expensive suit but I do recommend you make an effort to dress smartly. Having said that, if you do decide to wear a smart suit or formal outfit make sure it is clean and pressed. You can still look scruffy in a suit;

- Personal hygiene is all part and parcel of RAF life. Don't attend the interview unwashed, dirty or fresh from the building site!

- When you walk into the interview room, stand up straight with your shoulders back. Project an image of confidence and be polite, courteous and respectful to the interviewer at all times;

- Don't sit down in the interview chair until invited to do so. This will display good manners;

- Whilst you are in the interview chair sit upright with your hands resting on your knees, palms facing downwards. It is OK to use your hands expressively, but don't overdo it;

- Don't slouch in the chair. At the end of each question readjust your position;

- Whilst responding to the interview questions make sure you speak up and be positive. You will need to demonstrate a level of motivation and enthusiasm during the interview;

- Go the extra mile and learn a little bit about the RAF's history. When the panel ask you "What can you tell us about the Royal Air Force?" you will be able to demonstrate that you have made an effort to look into their history as well as their modern day activities;

- Ask positive questions at the end of the interview. Don't ask questions such as "How much leave will I get?" or "How often do I get paid?"

- If you are unsure about a question, try not to 'waffle'. If you do not know the answer, then it is OK to say so. Move on to the next question and put it behind you;

- Finally, believe in yourself and be confident.

CHAPTER 3
THE OASC
SCORING CRITERIA

Before I go onto explain the scoring criteria, let us first of all take a look at the competencies required to successfully pass Initial Officer Training (IOT).

Competencies Required for Success During Initial Officer Training

Interpersonal Competencies

Communication	Communicates accurately and effectively, orally and in writing.
Teamwork	Works willingly with others to achieve common goals.
Influence	Persuades others to follow a certain course of action.

Problem Solving Competencies

Appreciation	Comprehends, identifies, extracts and assimilates information from a range of sources, quickly and accurately.
Reasoning	Thinks logically, practically and coherently to produce a successful or reasonable solution, quickly and accurately.
Organisation	Determines priorities and allocates resources effectively and efficiently to a task(s).
Capacity	Holds and processes multiple inputs whilst maintaining task performance.

Character Competencies

Decisiveness	Makes sound appropriate decisions within time-scale demanded by the situation.
Self-motivation	Demonstrates a high level of commitment and interest to tasks.
Self-analysis	Monitors and objectively analyses own performance.
Integrity	Behaviour is guided by principles, morals and ethics appropriate to service life. Adheres to rules and regulations specific to RAF.

Now that we understand the competencies that are required to pass Initial Officer Training, we can explore the assessable qualities required and how they are linked in order to successfully pass the Officer and Aircrew Selection Centre (OASC).

The Competencies Assessed During OASC
Group & Individual Exercises Phase

COMPETENCY	DESCRIPTORS
Oral Communication	Delivery; effectiveness/understanding; listening.
Teamwork	Working with others; treatment of others; effort.
Influence	Impact on others; directing; persuasiveness.
Problem Solving	Judgement/reasoning; flexibility; comprehension; capacity; decisiveness.
Confidence and Resilience	Self assurance; composure; perseverance; assertion.

The RAF use what is known as a 'Behavioural Anchored Rating Scale' (BARS), which allows the assessors to rate a candidate's performance on a scale linked to clearly defined observable behaviours.

An example of a BAR is as follows:

ORAL COMMUNICATION

Standard - GRADE 4 (Good)

Delivery
Forceful projection, clear delivery.

Effectiveness / Understanding
Concise, succinct, articulate, lucid, easily understood, uses language/style appropriate to audience.

Listening
Listening to others' views attentively, asks patient questions to clarify.

Standard - GRADE 3 (Acceptable)

Delivery
Expresses self clearly, good pace, good projection.

Effectiveness / Understanding
Coherent, understandable, covers all points, comprehensive brief, speaks fluently.

Listening
Listening to others' suggestions.

Standard - GRADE 2 (Requires development)

Delivery
Makes himself/herself heard, projection varies, projection ok but drops, slight tendency to mumble, is quiet under pressure.

Effectiveness / Understanding
Covers most points, team didn't always understand, not concise lengthy briefs, inappropriate language – sense of occasion, rapid delivery, slight ponderous speech, disjointed brief, sometimes had to repeat brief.

Listening
Listens to major contributors in the group only.

Standard - GRADE 1 (Weak)

Delivery
Mumbles, mutters, monotonous, voice does not carry, whispers, barely audible, tends to slur words.

Effectiveness / Understanding
Monosyllabic, wooden, rambles, meaningless chatter, verbose, garrulous, struggles forming sentences, couldn't understand what his/her point was.

Listening
Doesn't listen to others' views, talks over others, and interrupts.

It is clear from the above BAR that you need to be aiming for 3's and 4's and should structure your communication around these areas. Look at Grade's 1 and 2 and avoid these actions!

When the Core Competencies are Assessed

The following information provides you with clear information as to when each area is assessed.

Confidence and Resilience – Assessed during every stage.

Oral Communication – Assessed during every stage.

Influence – Assessed during every stage with the exception of the Individual

Problem Solving exercise.

Problem Solving – Assessed during every stage with the exception of the discussion exercise.

Teamwork – Assessed during every stage with the exception of the discussion and the individual problem solving exercise.

You can begin to understand now why it is not important to find out what tasks you are going to undertake during the OASC. What is important is how you perform and behave in accordance with the Personal Qualities and the Core Competencies being assessed. As you can see from the table below, your scores from the Part 1 OASC interview will form part of the Overall Total Score. It is essential that during the Part 1 OASC interview you manage to meet the Personal Qualities that are being assessed.

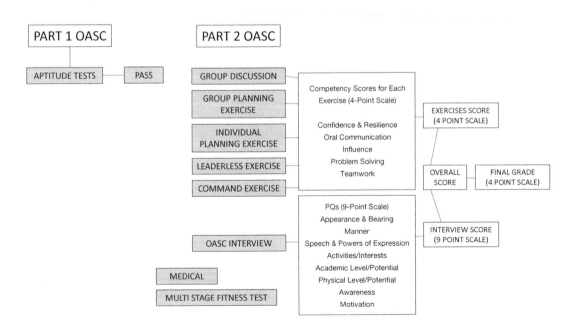

Tips for Passing the Oasc Interview

Appearance and bearing

This speaks for itself. Whilst at the OASC you are being watched all of the time, it is important that you conduct yourself in the correct manner. This means always looking smart, formal and speaking maturely.

Engage in conversation with the other candidates but do not mess around and draw unnecessary attention to yourself! During the interview sit up right in the interview chair, speak clearly, logically and concisely.

TOP TIP

During the first evening, go to officer's mess for a drink with the other candidates. Whilst I advise against having too much alcohol, one drink will do you no harm. Being able to socialise is all part and parcel of RAF life. Those people who sit in their room studying and cramming for the following days assessments might just fail the entire OASC! Your prep work should have been done well before you attend the OASC.

Manners

Be polite and courteous at all times. Be confident but do not cross the line of cockiness or arrogance!

Speech and power of expression

Be a fluent speaker. Be able to speak coherently, concisely, audibly and logically.

Activities and interests

Have plenty. Be rounded. Don't just be into fitness but have other interests too. If you are a volunteer for the ATC or you play a musical instrument, then this will work in your favour.

Academic level / potential

This should speak for itself, but make sure that you possess some academic qualities that give you an edge. Try and beat the bare minimum!

Physical level /potential

Be all round fit. Be able to achieve a good score on the bleep test and have a good level of stamina and strength.

Awareness

Know what's going on around you. Be up to date with current affairs and be aware of the life within the RAF and what it entails. Live and breathe the RAF whilst you are going through selection.

Motivation

This can make up for other areas that you are weak in. If you are highly motivated to join the RAF as an Officer, then this will shine through during selection. If you really want this, then tell them so!

Tips for Passing the OASC Exercises – Meeting the Core Competencies

During Part 2 OASC you will be assessed against the 5 leadership competencies as discussed previously. It is essential that you can meet each of these in order to have any chance of progressing. This stage will also include your medical and fitness test.

Confidence and Resilience

Be strong and stand by your decisions. Don't come across over confident but have an air of ability and sureness about you. The RAF wants to employ confident people.

Oral Communication

See the note previously that relates to the BARs and aim for 3's and 4's.

Influence

Have the power to influence others. If you have a good plan or ideas, then sell it to the others in the group. Don't just sit back and go with the flow if you believe it is wrong. As an RAF Officer you will need to influence your team in order to lead them effectively. Be confident in your ideas but DO NOT bully people.

Problem Solving

Think on your feet. This can only come with experience. Try to think 'out of the box' and look at the end goal/aim.

Teamwork

Have the ability to work with others.

CHAPTER 4
ABOUT THE
APTITUDE TESTS

The aptitude tests are perhaps the most difficult part of the selection process, and success in them will guarantee you have the opportunity to demonstrate your full potential. This chapter offers an explanation of each test, helping you familiarise yourself with what will be expected of you on the day.

Please note, these Computer Based Assessment Tests (CBAT) are only required for certain job positions, and therefore you may not be asked to undertake these assessments.

Psychomotor A

This test is designed to assess your hand and eye co-ordination. If you are applying to join the RAF as a pilot, then you will need to score well in this assessment.

During the test you are required to move a dot (which you control via a control stick) over a number of other circles. The circles themselves descend from the top of the screen, continuing downwards in a 'snake like' fashion. You will have the facility to practice this test before the real one commences. This practice session will allow you to familiarise yourself with the controls. To score maximum marks it is suggested you take the path which has the most descending circles and try and be as accurate as possible placing your dot over them. A steady hand is vital so avoid coffee and alcohol in the build up to the OASC.

Try playing computer games in the build up to the OASC as this will allow you to improve you hand/eye co-ordination.

Psychomotor B

The Psychomotor B test will also assess a candidates hand and eye co-ordination.

At the commencement of the test a cross and a red dot will appear. Your task is to keep the dot as close to the centre of the cross as possible. As you can imagine, a steady hand is imperative during this test. Just like Psychomotor A, you will use a control stick in order to move the red dot up and down. You will also be required to use your feet to move the dot from left to right. Moving the control stick from left to right has no effect on the red dot.

Once again you will be permitted to carry out a practice run in order to get used to the weight and feel of the hand and foot controls.

Try playing computer games in the build up to the OASC as this will allow you to improve your hand/eye coordination.

Digit Recall

Digital recall is used to assess your memory. A series of digits will appear on a computer screen for a period of 5 seconds. You must study the digits intently for the 5 seconds as it will be your task to re-enter the digits, in the correct order, once they disappear. The number of digits that will appear, and consequently you have to remember, will gradually increase up to 15.

You are advised to remember as many digits as possible, rather than trying to remember all 15. For example, if a row of 15 digits appear on the screen, focus on remembering the first 10 as opposed to the entire sequence.

During the second part of this test you will be required to memorise how many different 'types' of each number appear on the screen. For example, the number sequence 55686254351 may appear for a 5 second period. Once the 5 seconds is up, the screen will go blank and it is your job to answer a specific question, such as – How many number 5's were in the sequence.

TOP TIPS: practice by remembering telephone numbers and car registration plates.

Numerical Reasoning

This test assesses your ability to understand and interpret numerical information as well as performing simple mathematical calculations. You will be presented with tables of numerical information. It is your task to analyse the information and data before answering a series of questions. There will be 4 tables and 16 questions in total.

TOP TIP

Use online numerical reasoning practice tests at the following website:
www.How2Become.com.

Verbal Reasoning

In this test you are presented with multiple screen shots containing 7 to 9 short passages of text. You are given approximately 3 minutes reading time to take in all the information available. You are then asked several questions which you will have to combine information from multiple passages to answer. The interface allows you to view two passages on the screen at once, one in the upper part of the screen in a red box and another in the lower part of screen in a green box.

Detailed instructions are provided - make sure that you thoroughly read the information in the short passages.

TOP TIP

Use online verbal reasoning practice tests at the following website:
www.How2Become.com

Mat-A

This test comes in two separate parts. During the first part of the test you will be provided with a sheet of laminated paper which includes a table of data. There will be rows of -25 to 25 and columns of -15 to 15. You are then provided with row coordinates and column coordinates. You will then be required to find the value which is contained within a particular square before inputting the information into a computer. For example row -21, column 6, may have a value of 18, therefore you would input 18 into the computer screen.

Part two is slightly different to Part 1 in the fact that you are provided with more information. On the other side of the laminated paper are four tables, each table provides information on speed, altitude, angle, drift and ground speed. Using these tables you will be expected to cross reference data to find a value. You will have to interpret whichever tables are relevant to answer the question asked.

Mat-B

This test involves general maths questions with the primary focus on speed, distance and time (SDT) calculations. To prepare for these you need to revise quick mental maths and simple algebra.

TOP TIP

Visit the following website for some free SDT calculations:
www.SpeedDistanceTime.info.

Vigilance

During the vigilance you will be assessed against your 'awareness'. You will be presented with a 9x9 grid which has a number of stars/asterisks spread across it.

The requirement of this test is to cancel each star/asterisk by entering the correct coordinates into the computer. Note: As soon as you enter the coordinates they cannot be altered. As well as the stars/asterisks, every 5-15 seconds a red arrow appears in a grid. The red arrow is a priority task which must be cancelled out before you can continue with the stars/asterisks. To cancel out the red arrow, you just need to enter the coordinates into the computer. You will then be able to continue dealing with the remaining asterisks.

TOP TIP

Don't try and cross out asterisks all over the grid, concentrate on a few rows.

Clan

This assesses your ability to multi-task.

1. Red, yellow and green diamonds move from the left into coloured bands. When they reach the coloured band you must 'cancel' them using the coloured buttons. This only works when the diamond is completely within the band, if even a tip is out, it will not register. Wrong or surplus keys used here lose 1 point, correct keys gain 1 point.

2. Simple mathematical problems appear at the bottom of the screen, involving addition, subtraction, multiplication and division of numbers 1-12, 15 and 20. Each correct answer gives 1 point, wrong answers lose 1 point.

3. Every 15-20 seconds, 5-9 alphanumeric digits appear at the top for a few seconds. 12 seconds later, four similar options are presented at each corner of the screen; you must select the option which appeared previously using A/B/C/D.

TOP TIP

Practice basic arithmetic at the following website: www.thatquiz.org.

Navigation

The main part of the screen has a flight plan (map) with 5-8 turning points and distances. At the side of this part of the screen is three coloured buttons. Each button opens 2 to 3 tables which show the aircrafts speed against weight load and fuel consumption against speed (units are measured in miles per minute or miles per gallon, and equations are given). You are given two minutes to study the tables and maps after this time questions will appear (5 or 10 per section) in which you have 1 minute to answer the question.

The questions usually specify a route of two legs, perhaps carrying a certain weight and with winds increasing/decreasing the speed of the aircraft. The numbers do not always divide exactly, so estimation and rounding are essential. Later sections involve more than one possible aircraft. Questions include finding arrival time, departure time, fuel consumed, fuel left, perhaps with new distances/times/fuel. Points are given for close estimates.

Instrument Comprehension A

In this test you are presented with an artificial horizon showing attitude and bank (markers at 30 and 60 degrees), and a compass showing direction. You are given five possible aircraft attitudes (they are red arrow hawks). The objective is to select the aircraft attitude that reflects the instruments. North is represented by the aircraft going away from you, South by the aircraft coming towards you, East by the aircraft pointing right, West by the aircraft pointing left. There are 25 questions, which progressively become more difficult.

TOP TIP

Imagine you are in the aircraft (how would the aircraft and instruments look), learn flight instruments and what they do (flight simulators may help in this instance) military flight aptitude books have similar examples of this kind of test.

Instrument Comprehension B

As in Instrument Comprehension A, you are given an artificial horizon with a compass. This time an altimeter, air speed indicator and turn/slip indicator also appear. In this test there are five descriptions of aircraft for you to choose from. Descriptions are roughly as follows: Aircraft travelling WSW at 270kts, nose up, ascending through 1,500ft in sharp bank to the left. You must select which description most closely matches the aircrafts instruments presented in front of you.

TOP TIP
Use one instrument initially to filter the options and then add more instruments for detail.

Visual Search

This test is in two parts; the first using letters, the second using symbols. A grid of letters or symbols is given, starting at an approximate size of 3x4 squares. You are given a letter or symbol to locate in the grid, and when you have found it you must enter its 2-digit grid location, using the numeric keypad. Every few answers, the grid size increases. This is a speed test, and it helps if you can use the numeric keypad on a keyboard without looking at it.

Spatial Reasoning

To begin with a red spitfire enters a 3D projection and performs manoeuvres including left/right (yaws) and nose-up/down. Each manoeuvre is assigned a key on your keyboard. You must follow the spitfire through its manoeuvres, having 2 seconds to press the relevant key for the movement the aircraft is making. You are given a short practise session, in which the key inputs are registered. As the test advances more spitfires enter the screen and sometimes swap colours. You must always follow the red spitfire.

TOP TIP
Imagine you are the pilot and input the actions as if you were him/her. For example if the aircraft is coming towards and moves to the right of the screen, the aircraft is actually turning left.

Spatial Memory

This test uses the same screen format as the spatial reasoning test. During the test there are six different coloured spitfires performing manoeuvres whilst flying in and out of the screen area. You are then asked questions about the positions/manoeuvres that were performed, with 4 possible colours of aircraft to choose from.

Examples include:
- Which aircraft performed a complete loop?
- Which aircraft was flying in the opposite direction to the BLUE aircraft at the end of the simulation?
- Which was the first aircraft to enter the screen area?

Useful Websites

The following websites will provide you with some useful resources to assist you during your preparation for the RAF Officer aptitude tests:

www.speeddistancetime.info

www.rafofficeroasc.co.uk

CHAPTER 5
THE GROUP
DISCUSSION

The group discussion element of the OASC is designed to assess your ability to communicate and interact with other people. As you are already aware, RAF Officers are required to communicate, and discuss topical issues with other members of the RAF. In addition to this they must have the intellect to converse with agencies outside of the Armed Forces as well as their colleagues from the Army and the Royal Navy. This part of the assessment will determine your ability to do just that.

There will be up to eight people in the discussion which will be a mix of ages and genders. It is important that you can get on with everyone, regardless of their age, background, religious beliefs or sexual orientation. Before I provide you with some tips on how to score high during the group discussion, let us first of all revisit the scoring criteria. Out of the different assessable areas, the following will be assessed during the discussion:

- Confidence and Resilience;

- Oral Communication;

- Influence.

Many candidates believe that all you need to do during the discussion in order to score well is to contribute to the discussion. This couldn't be further from the truth. Yes it is imperative that you get involved and have an opinion, but you must concentrate on other areas too, such as your ability to listen to others and involve others in the conversation. You will see that one of the assessable areas is that of 'influence'. During the discussion, you may be presented with a situation where the other members of the group disagree with your opinion or view. Whilst that is fine and acceptable, would you be able to influence them and change their mind about your views?

Here are a number of important tips that will help you score high during the group discussion.

<u>Tip 1</u>

Whilst in the chair, sit up-right and do not slouch or lean forward. Sit with your legs uncrossed and rest your palms on your knees. Whilst you should not sit rigid, you should look presentable.

Tip 2

There will be a number of discussions to be had. In total the discussion session will last for approximately 40 minutes, so there is ample time for you to get involved and score high. Try starting off a few discussions. Don't just leave it to the other members of the group to start off the topic. Remember, one of the assessable areas is that of confidence and resilience.

If you are struggling to think of anything to say for a specific topic, you could start off the conversation by saying:

"Does anybody have any strong views on this topic?"

By saying this, you will be actively involved in the conversation and you will be also involving others into the conversation.

Tip 3

When you have finished contributing to the debate, try and involve another person into the conversation. For example:

"That's my view on this subject, what do you think?"

Once again you will score higher marks for actively involving others into the conversation.

Tip 4

Involve other people who have not yet had chance to speak. If you notice a member of the group struggling to get their opinion heard, try saying something like:

"I notice you haven't had the chance to say anything yet, what's your view on this subject?"

Tip 5

Actively demonstrate good listening skills. This is the part that many people are poor at. Once they have finished speaking, they sit back and wait for their turn to speak again. Avoid this at all costs! I strongly recommend that you show active listening skills when other people in the group are speaking. Nod your head and use facial expressions to demonstrate that you are still involved in the topic of conversation.

Tip 6

Be careful what you say! Over the past few years I have run a number of 1 day RAF Officer training courses that help people prepare for their OASC. During the course we run through a number of group discussions. During every session, someone is guaranteed to say something that will probably give them an automatic fail for the entire OASC! Sometimes people have a tendency to say something controversial; albeit they probably didn't intend to. My advice is this – it is important that you get involved during the discussions, and even more important that you have an opinion and don't sit on the fence. However, you must think before you speak. If you believe that what you will say might be taken in the wrong way, avoid saying it.

Tip 7

Speak clearly and concisely. During the group discussion be clear in what you say, speak up and avoid hesitations such as 'erm' or 'agh'. In addition to other areas, you are being assessed on your oral communication skills.

Tip 8

Have a number of topics that you can start off a discussion with. Although it is more probable that the assessing staff will provide you the topics to discuss, they may also ask you to come up with topics yourself. Therefore, before you attend OASC, pick 5 subjects that you can use during the group discussions phase.

Now let's take a look at a number of sample topics that have been used in the past.

Sample Group Discussion Topics

- *Should women be allowed to join the Armed Forces?*

- *Was Hitler a good leader?*

- *What do you think about gay people being allowed to join the Armed Forces?*

- *Speeding cameras are a total waste of time – discuss.*

- *How could the use and popularity of public transport be increased within this country?*

- *Professional footballers. Are they overpaid?*

- *Is the increase in overseas football club owners good for the sport?*

- *The pros and cons of having a credit card.*

- *Marijuana has a medical value.*

- *The pros and cons of a female President.*

- *Should schools distribute condoms?*

- *Life imprisonment is a good alternative to capital punishment.*

- *What makes a good leader?*

- *Was the Iraq war a waste of time?*

- *What should Britain's place in Europe be?*

- *Is modern technology changing the way we communicate for the better?*

- *Should smoking have been banned in public places?*

- *Is animal testing defensible in modern society?*

- *Should the public be concerned about the increasing use of DNA technology?*

- *Should people be required to opt out of organ donation rather than opt in?*

- *How could more people be encouraged to vote?*

- *Can the salaries of professional football players be justified?*

- *Should the private life of celebrities come under so much scrutiny?*
- *Do we need to change the attitude of car drivers towards speed limits?*
- *Should our police officers be routinely armed?*
- *Should we be worried about obesity?*
- *Should organised team sport be included in the national curriculum?*
- *Should there be a compulsory retirement age?*
- *Do we need to change Britain's drinking culture?*
- *Should there be any limitations to the treatment available on the NHS?*
- *Has the National Lottery been good for Britain?*
- *Should the BBC be funded by a license fee?*

CHAPTER 6
PREPARING
FOR THE PLANNING
EXERCISES

Group Planning Exercise

Each syndicate member is given a copy of the exercise setting, some rough paper and a pencil. The setting, chosen from a number available, contains a map and the brief of an imaginary situation which the syndicate team has found itself in. There are normally two or more possible solutions to the problem and the aim is for the syndicate to arrive at a group-preferred solution. The exercise is divided into three phases:

The Private Study Period

After the briefing, you are given 15 minutes for private study during which you are expected to acquaint yourself with the brief and setting, making whatever notes you wish and undertaking your own speed/distance/time calculations to arrive at one or more solutions.

The Discussion Period

Next, a 20-minute period is given for the group to discuss the options, check calculations and arrive at a team solution. No chairman is appointed and discussion is on a free-for-all basis. During this phase, the Board, who takes no active part in the discussion, will assess which members of the syndicate have influence, perception, comprehension and judgement and a note is made of their degree of involvement, cooperation and numeracy of each member.

The Question Period

There then follows a 20-25 minute phase during which the Board Chairman questions each member of the syndicate about the setting, the problem, the chosen solution, the rejected solutions and the calculations. By the end of the questioning, the Board Member, who will have been marking throughout this period, will have noted the qualities apparent in each syndicate member (as well as confirming, or otherwise, those qualities already noted as above), in addition to mental agility, flexibility and reaction to pressure.

Individual Planning Exercise

This exercise is similar in nature to the Group Planning exercise, and the scenario is selected from a number of options which the Boarding Officers posses. You have 20 minutes to understand and assess the problem, undertake calculations and decide which solution to present. You are then questioned for 10 minutes by a Board Member.

You will be questioned on the problem, your solution and the alternatives you considered. While the candidate is being questioned, the Board Chairman is engaged in assessing the level of performance, commenting on confidence, work rate, perception, judgement, comprehension and numeracy. The Board Member then leads the candidate through the possible alternatives and further assessment is based on receptiveness, flexibility, judgement, mental agility, composure, reaction to pressure, and decisiveness. At the end of the question period, the Board discusses the performance and awards a percentage score. This continues until each member of the syndicate has been seen.

The Board President observes the performance of each candidate remotely by CCTV and makes his own judgement and assessments. Clearly, he is unable to observe each candidate's performance in full, but he spends sufficient time on each candidate to form an opinion. Any major differences of opinion as to the qualities possessed by any candidate are discussed at the final debrief between the President and the Board Members.

Top tips for scoring high during the group/individual planning:

• Demonstrate strength of character.

• Don't give in, even if things are going wrong.

• Support your decision and consider all eventualities.

• Improve general arithmetic and be competent in the use of speed, distance and time (SDT).

• Be able to calculate SDT questions in your head, as well as being able to write them down. You can practice by getting a member of your family to ask you a series of SDT questions. This is great practice as you will be under pressure to answer the questions without the use of a calculator, pen and paper.

• Keep an eye on the time. You need to come up with a solution to the problem.

- Be alert and quick to respond to questions.
- Never lie when answering questions from the assessors, they will see straight through it. If you do not know the answer to a question, then just say so.
- Always remain calm. The questioning at the end of the exercise is designed to be tough and assess how well you cope under pressure.

Speed, Distance and Time

Accuracy and agility in speed, distance, and time calculations will help you perform well during the RAF Officer selection process. The following information will assist you in understanding how to tackle these type of questions.

When trying to solve these problems it is important to consider three variables: speed, distance and time. Try not to get too worried as two of these variables will always be known. The easiest way to solve these equations is to use the following formulas:

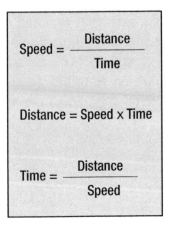

$$\text{Speed} = \frac{\text{Distance}}{\text{Time}}$$

$$\text{Distance} = \text{Speed} \times \text{Time}$$

$$\text{Time} = \frac{\text{Distance}}{\text{Speed}}$$

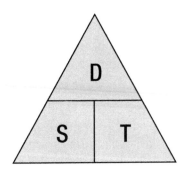

The triangular diagram above is ideal for helping you to remember the formula. Simply place your finger over the variable you are trying to discover, you will then see the equation required.

For example if you wanted to obtain the time, placing your finger on 'T' would show that you would need to divide distance (D) by speed (S).

Let's now work through some examples:

1. A train travels 60 miles in 3 hours. What is the train's speed?

Formula: Speed = distance ÷ time

Speed = 60 ÷ 3 = 20 mph

2. A car is travelling at 30 mph for 70 minutes. What is the distance travelled?

With this problem it is important to remember to work in minutes!

So, 30 mph = 0.5 miles per minute (30 ÷ 60)

70 (minutes) × 0.5 = 35 miles

You can use the formula but you need to convert the minutes into hours and remember that 0.1 = 1/10 of 60 minutes:

Formula: Distance = speed × time

Distance = 30 × 1.1666r (1 hour 10 mins) = 35

3. A tank is driving at 48 mph over 60 miles. How long was it driving for?

Formula: Time = distance ÷ speed

Time = 60 ÷ 48 = 1 hour 15 minutes

Take these steps

1. You know that 48 mph = 48 miles in 60 minutes.
2. The difference between 60 and 48 is 12, which is ¼ of 48.
3. You can then take ¼ of 60, which gives 15 minutes, and add that to 60 minutes = 75 minutes.
4. Then convert to hours = 1 hour 15 minutes for the answer!

OR

Take these steps

1. You know that 48 mph = 0.8 miles per minute.
2. 60 ÷ 0.8 = 75 minutes.
3. Convert into hours = 1 hour 15 minutes.

Once you understand how to calculate speed, distance and time, take your time to work through the 30 sample test questions that follow.

In order to obtain further Speed, Distance and Time questions, and also try 8 planning exercises, please go to: www.How2Become.com

Sample Speed, Distance, and Time Test Questions

(Give all distances and speeds in whole numbers)

Question 1

You are travelling at 28 mph for 75 minutes. How far do you travel?

Answer

Question 2

You travel 15 miles in half an hour. What speed are you travelling at?

Answer

Question 3

You travel 33 miles at a constant speed of 55 mph. How long are you travelling for?

Answer

Question 4

You are travelling at 75 mph for 1 and half hours. How far do you travel?

Answer

Question 5

You travel 61 miles in 1 hour and 5 minutes. What speed are you travelling at?

Answer

Question 6

You travel 90 miles at a constant speed of 30 mph. How long are you travelling for?

Answer [   ]

Question 7

You are travelling at 70 mph for 126 minutes. How far do you travel?

Answer [   ]

Question 8

You travel 2.5 miles in 5 minutes. What speed are you travelling at?

Answer [   ]

Question 9

You travel 75 miles at a constant speed of 45 mph. How long are you travelling for?

Answer [   ]

Question 10

You are travelling at 60 mph for quarter of an hour. How far do you travel?

Answer [   ]

Question 11

You travel 325 miles in 4 hours and 6 minutes. What speed are you travelling at?

Answer

Question 12

You travel 39 miles at 45 mph. How long are you travelling for?

Answer

Question 13

You are travelling at 80 mph for 15 minutes. How far do you travel?

Answer

Question 14

You travel 63 miles in 54 minutes. What speed are you travelling at?

Answer

Question 15

You travel 20 miles at 50 mph. How long are you travelling for?

Answer

Question 16

You are travelling at 65 mph for 1 hour and 12 minutes. How far do you travel?

Answer

Question 17

You travel 120 miles in 2 hours. What speed are you travelling at?

Answer

Question 18

You travel 80 miles at 50 mph. How long are you travelling for?

Answer

Question 19

You are travelling at 40 mph for half an hour. How far do you travel?

Answer

Question 20

You travel 80 miles in 1 hour and 40 minutes. What speed are you travelling at?

Answer

Question 21

You travel 35 miles at 70 mph. How long are you travelling for?

Answer

Question 22

You are travelling at 15 mph for 8 minutes. How far do you travel?

Answer

Question 23

You travel 16 miles in quarter of an hour. What speed are you travelling at?

Answer

Question 24

You travel 60 miles at 50 mph. How long are you travelling for?

Answer

Question 25

You are travelling at 30 mph for 10 minutes. How far do you travel?

Answer

Question 26

You travel 75 miles in one and half hours. What speed are you travelling at?

Answer

Question 27

You travel 1 mile at 60 mph. How long are you travelling for?

Answer

Question 28

You are travelling at 50 mph for 2 and half hours. How far do you travel?

Answer

Question 29

You travel 100 miles in 1 hour and 20 minutes. What speed are you travelling at?

Answer

Question 30

You travel 600 miles at 80 mph. How long are you travelling for?

Answer

Answers

1. 35 miles	**16.** 78 miles
2. 30 mph	**17.** 60 mph
3. 36 mins	**18.** 1 hour 36 mins
4. 112.5 miles	**19.** 20 miles
5. 56 mph	**20.** 48 mph
6. 3 hours	**21.** 30 mins
7. 147 miles	**22.** 2 miles
8. 30 mph	**23.** 64 mph
9. 1hour 40 minutes	**24.** 1 hour 12 mins
10. 15 miles	**25.** 5 miles
11. 79 mph	**26.** 50 mph
12. 52 mins	**27.** 1 minute
13. 20 miles	**28.** 125 miles
14. 70 mph	**29.** 75 mph
15. 24 mins	**30.** 7 hours 30 minutes

On the following pages I have provided you with a sample planning exercise for you to try. Give it a go and see how you get on. There is no time limit for this sample exercise.

Planning Exercise - Seaside Mission

You are the duty officer in charge at the Royal National Lifeboat Institution's (RNLI) rescue centre at FLITTERBY. The FLITTERBY lifeboat is currently involved in rescuing some sailors from a drifting yacht in the Irish Sea.

It is exactly 10:00 am and the coxswain of the lifeboat has just radioed the following message to you:

"One of the sailors we have taken off from the sinking yacht is desperately ill and must have a blood transfusion as soon as possible. I have just been talking, by radio, to the Accident & Emergency (A&E) staff at ASHBY hospital and they will be standing-by to receive him but have pointed out that every minute counts. Make sure the RNLI's ambulance (a specially adapted estate car) is ready to take him to the hospital as soon as we arrive at the jetty. I cannot give you an exact time of arrival, but it will not be before 10:20 hours, or later than 10:45 hours. Once we are tied up, it will take us 5 minutes to get him from the boat into the ambulance. It will be up to you to get him from the jetty to the A&E dept with the utmost urgency."

You study the map and recollect that there are 3 ways to get to hospital, each with advantages and disadvantages:

Seaside Mission Sketch

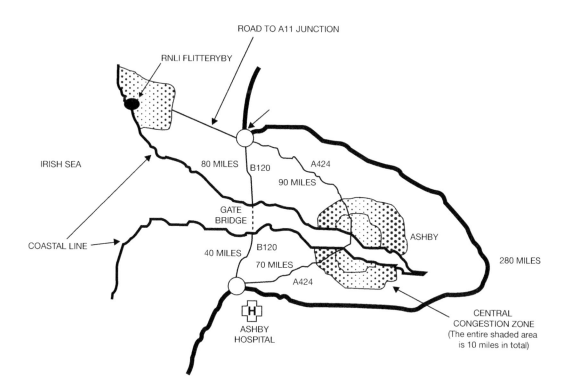

1. The route via the gate bridge is subject to delays as the crossings are controlled and the bridge is only open 3 times per hour for 12 minutes. The bridge is open at 10 minutes past, 30 minutes past and 10 minutes to the hour. The journey across the gate bridge will take you 10 minutes. The B120 is twisty and a maximum average speed could be no greater than 40 mph.

2. The route through the centre of ASHBY on the A424 is further but although it should be possible to average 40 mph out of town, once inside the central congestion zone, heavy traffic and narrow streets means no more than 5 mph can be averaged for the 10 miles through the walled part of the town. The one limitation from using the A424 is that from 11:00 hrs onwards the central congestion zone is very dense and traffic is at a standstill.

3. The new A11 by-pass is dual carriage and passes the hospital but, although the longest route, will allow averages of 70 mph to be achieved. It is possible to reach the A11 from FLITTERBY in 10 mins.

You warn the duty driver to stand-by. Unfortunately, you cannot alert the local police on the telephone to make any special arrangements, so there is no way of interrupting the steady but reliable timetable of the gate bridge. The duty officer at nearby RAF Valley tells you the Search and Rescue helicopter is unavailable as it is on a mission rescuing someone from an oil rig miles out to sea.

Your aim is to transport the sailor to the hospital in the quickest time possible.

Question 1

How long in minutes will it take you to get from RNLI Flitterby to the A11 junction?

Answer

Question 2

Based on the sailor arriving at Flitterby at the earliest time possible, what time will you reach the Hospital if you choose route 1?

Answer

Question 3

Based on the sailor arriving at Flitterby at the latest time possible, what time will you reach the Hospital if you choose route 3?

Answer

Question 4

Based on the sailor arriving at Flitterby at the latest time possible, what time will you reach the Hospital if you choose route 1?

Answer

Question 5

Based on the sailor arriving at Flitterby at the earliest time possible, what time will you reach the Hospital if you choose route 2?

Answer

NOTE - You are to calculate the total journey times for each of the 3 different routes using Speed, Distance and Time calculations.

Your Calculations

Remember:

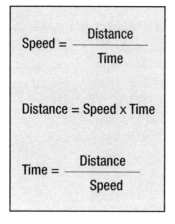

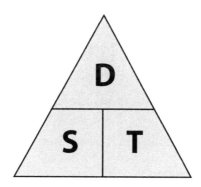

Answers to Planning Exercises

Question 1

How long in minutes will it take you to get from RNLI Flitterby to the A11 junction?

ANSWER: 10 minutes

Question 2

Based on the sailor arriving at Flitterby at the earliest time possible, what time will you reach the Hospital if you choose route 1?

The sailor arrives at Flitterby at 10:20hrs. It takes 5 minutes to load him into the ambulance which brings the time to 10:25hrs. It takes 10 minutes to get to the A11 junction which brings the time to 10:35hrs.

Travelling route 1, it is a total of 80 miles to the Gate Bridge. We are able to travel at a maximum speed of 40mph. To find out the time it takes to travel this distance we need to use the following calculation:

Time = Distance / Speed
Time = 80 / 40

ANSWER: 2 hours

We now know that we will arrive at the Gate Bridge at 12:35hrs. From the information provided we know that the Gate Bridge is open 3 times per hour for 12 minutes. The bridge is open at 10 minutes past, 30 minutes past and 10 minutes to the hour.

The bridge is already open when we arrive at 12:35 hours; therefore we are able to cross straight away. The journey across the gate bridge takes us 10 minutes, which means that we will arrive on the other side at 12:45hrs.

We now have to make the final journey along the B120 towards the hospital. The distance is 40 miles in total and we can travel at a maximum speed of 40 miles per hour. In order to calculate the time we need to use the following calculation:

Time = Distance / Speed
Time = 40 / 40

Answer = 1 hour

ANSWER: Arrive at the hospital at 13:45hrs.

Question 3

Based on the sailor arriving at Flitterby at the latest time possible, what time will you reach the Hospital if you choose route 3?

The sailor arrives at Flitterby at 10:45hrs. It takes 5 minutes to load him into the ambulance which brings the time to 10:50hrs. It takes 10 minutes to get to the A11 junction which brings the time to 11:00hrs.

Travelling along route 3 we know that we can achieve a maximum speed of 70 miles per hour. In order to work out the total time it will take us to reach the hospital we need to use the following calculation:

Time = Distance / Speed
Time = 280 / 70
Answer = 4 hours

ANSWER: Arrive at the hospital will be 15:00hrs.

Question 4

Based on the sailor arriving at Flitterby at the latest time possible, what time will you reach the Hospital if you choose route 1?

The sailor arrives at Flitterby at 10:45hrs. It takes 5 minutes to load him into the ambulance which brings the time to 10:50hrs. It takes 10 minutes to get to the A11 junction which brings the time to 11:00hrs.

Travelling route 1, it is a total of 80 miles to the Gate Bridge. We are able to travel at a maximum speed of 40mph. To find out the time it takes to travel this distance we need to use the following calculation:

Time = Distance / Speed
Time = 80 / 40
Answer = 2 hours

We now know that we will arrive at the Gate Bridge at 13:00hrs. From the information provided we know that the Gate Bridge is open 3 times per hour for 12 minutes. The bridge is open at 10 minutes past, 30 minutes past and 10 minutes to the hour.

The bridge is still open when we arrive at 13:00 hours; therefore we are able to cross straight away. The journey across the gate bridge takes us 10 minutes, which means that we will arrive on the other side at 13:10hrs.

We now have to make the final journey along the B120 towards the hospital. The distance is 40 miles in total and we can travel at a maximum speed of 40 miles per hour. In order to calculate the time we need to use the following calculation:

Time = Distance / Speed
Time = 40 / 40
Answer = 1 hour

ANSWER: Arrive at the hospital at 14:10hrs.

Question 5

Based on the sailor arriving at Flitterby at the earliest time possible, what time will you reach the Hospital if you choose route 2?

The sailor arrives at Flitterby at 10:20hrs. It takes 5 minutes to load him into the ambulance which brings the time to 10:25hrs. It takes 10 minutes to get to the A11 junction which brings the time to 10:35hrs.

We know that the distance from the A11 junction to the edge of the congestion zone is a total of 90 miles. We also know that the distance from the other side of the congestion zone to the hospital along the A424 is a total of 70 miles. Therefore we can add these two distances together to get a total distance (minus the congestion zone area) of 160 miles. In order to work out the time it takes to travel this distance we need to use the following calculation:

Time = Distance / Speed
Time = 160 / 40
Answer = 4 hours

We now need to work out the time it will take us to travel through the congestion zone. We know from the map that the distance inside the congestion zone is a total of 10 miles. We can only travel at a maximum speed of 5mph; therefore the calculation used to find out the total time it takes to travel through the congestion zone is as follows:

Time = Distance / Speed
Time = 10 / 5
Answer = 2 hours

All we need to do now is add the two travelling times together to reach a total of 6 hours travelling time.

ANSWER: Arrive at the hospital at 16:35hrs

Planning Exercise - Logistic Majestic

You are the dispatcher and driver for an Army Military Transport Unit based at UPSHOT BARRACKS (see attached map). Your normal operating hours are from 07:30 hours to whenever the last job is completed. However, this evening your Commanding Officer wants all members of the unit, in uniform, for a photograph at 17:05 hrs. Nonetheless, the unit directive requires that all requests for same-day transport received before 15:00 hours be met; after that time, tasks will be held over for the following day.

With 2 tasks left to complete today and the 15:00 hours deadline approaching, the telephone rings. A Royal Engineer, not affiliated to your unit is needed urgently at Garrick Barracks outside the town and he needs to take a large, bulky tank part with him. A lack of fuel, due to a petrol tanker drivers' strike, means that he can only get as far as your office so he needs onward travel; he will be with you any moment now and he expects to stay at Garrick barracks for 45 minutes. You already have a 150kg package to collect from one of your regular customers, a supply depot in RIGBY, to be delivered to the barracks next door to your office, and the wife of the Commanding Officer needs to be collected from home in HAMPTON by 15:25 hours to attend a civic reception in the Town Hall opposite the office at 15:45 hours.

Due to other tasks, the only vehicles now available to you are an estate car similar to that used by the specialist engineer and with 30 litres of fuel in the tank, a small truck with 17 litres and a courier motorcycle complete with panniers with 9 litres. In addition to you there are 2 other drivers available. The previously mentioned petrol strike means no further fuel is available. The estate car can average 30 mph at 2½ miles/litre; the truck can average 40 mph at 5 miles/litre and the motorcycle averages 50mph at 10miles/litre. You also know that major road-works south of the town will add 20 minutes to the direct journey between UPSHOT and RIGBY.

By the time you complete your plan and brief the other drivers it will be 15:00 hours. Find a solution that allows all tasks to be completed in the allotted time.

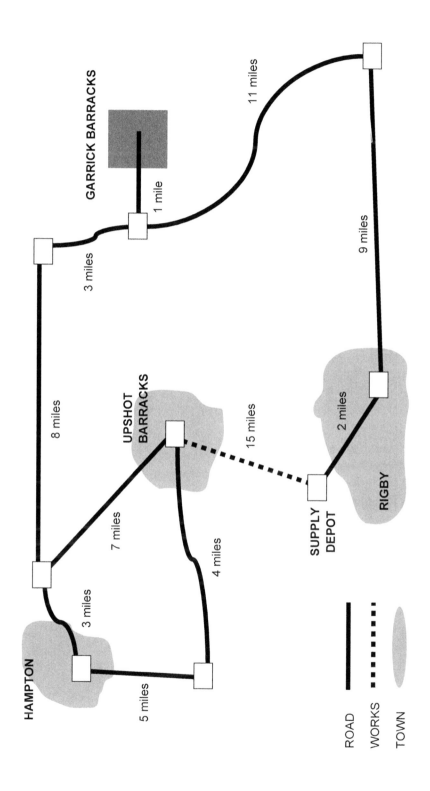

Logistic Majestic Solutions

IMPORTANT! The following solutions are just examples of a possible way to complete the tasks in hand. They do not represent the most efficient or quickest way to complete the exercise, and should be used for guidance only.

Aim

All tasks need to be completed and all personnel present for the unit photo at 1705 hours.

Factors & Plan

Estate cars movements

Estate car to Commanding Officer's house ETD 15:00 (10 miles at 30 mph = 20 mins).

- ETA 15:20 and departs at same time for Town Hall (another 10 miles at 30mph = 20 mins).

- ETA 15:40 (5 mins to spare unless departure was delayed to 15:05).

Estate car now departs to Garrick Barracks ETD 15:40 (19 miles at 30 mph = 38 mins)

- ETA 16:18, collects Royal engineer

Estate car returns to unit (19 miles at 30 mph = 38 mins)

- ETA 16:56

Trucks movements

Truck to Garrick Barracks with Royal Engineer ETD 15:00 (19 miles at 40 mph = 28 mins)

- ETA 15:28 – Royal Engineer will be ready to depart at 16:13

Truck to supply depot (via South East route) (23 miles at 40 mph = 34 mins)

- ETD 15:28 for supply depot

- ETA and ETD supply depot 16:03

Truck return to barracks via road works (15 miles at 40 mph – 22 mins)

- Add 20 mins for road works

- ETA 16:45

Motor cycle

If the Royal Engineer has fitted bulky tank part and has no part to return, he could be collected by the motor cycle and would not, therefore have the 4 min wait at Garrick Barracks. However, even his tools might not fit in the panniers.

Motor cycle to Garrick Barracks (ETD as required) (but at 15:50 if there was no wait by either party) (19 miles at 50 mph = 23 mins)

- ETA 16:13

Motor cycle back to Upshot Barracks (19 miles at 50 mph = 23 mins)

- ETA 16:36

Other Solutions

One option would be to send the motor cycle to the Station Commander's house, the Estate car to the depot and the truck to Garrick Barracks, where it waits for the engineer. The Station Commander would not be very happy with his wife being on a motor cycle, though! All 3 drivers are also used, so there is no one to take the orders for tomorrow's tasks.

A second option would be to take the engineer to Garrick Barracks by truck, which then drives on to the supply depot, returning to Garrick to pick up the engineer up by reverse route. The estate car could then be used for the Commanding Officer's wife. However, the truck would be late arriving back (ETA 17:06) and you are under orders to be ready for the photograph by 17:05.

CHAPTER 7
THE LEADERLESS
AND
COMMAND TASKS

During the Officer and Aircrew Selection Centre you will be required to undertake both a Leaderless task and also a Command task. Both tasks involve the solution of a 'practical' problem over an 'obstacle course'. In the Leaderless exercise there is no appointed leader whereas in the Command Situation exercise each candidate takes a turn as leader and must direct the rest of the syndicate.

Let's now take a look at how you can achieve higher marks in each of the tasks.

The Leaderless Task

As the name suggests, this task is performed without a designated leader. The purpose of the assessment is to see how effective you are at working as part of a team and also to identify those people who have leadership potential. Those people who do have leadership potential will naturally come to the front and move the completion of the task forward.

As part of your group you will be provided with a task that must be completed within a set piece of time. The task might be a requirement for your group to move an object from point A to B, with certain restrictions in place, such as avoiding an area of floor space or only using specific items of equipment. Whatever the task/brief, it is important that you work effectively as a team member and try to come up with solutions to the problem.

Before I provide you with a number of tips to help you score higher during the leaderless task, let's take a look at a number of key areas that are essential to the smooth running of any task.

Component 1 – Time

It is important that any team working towards a common goal is aware of the time constraints. Make sure everyone is aware of the time and keep checking it regularly if the facility exists.

Component 2 – Plan

Every team that is working towards a common goal should have a plan in place. If you don't have a plan, how are you going to achieve the task in hand? The way to compile a successful plan is to ask the team if they have any ideas on how the task could be achieved.

Component 3 – Communication

This is probably the most important component of any team task. Communication means talking to, and listening to, the other members of the team. Get this part wrong and the task is guaranteed to fail.

Component 4 – Allocation of tasks

Everybody in the team will have different 'strengths'. You should try to find out who is good at what, and then allocate tasks accordingly.

Component 5 – Support

It is the duty of every team member to support the other members of the team.

Component 6 – URGENCY!

Regardless of how long you have to complete the task, urgency is a must.

Now let's take a look at a number of tips that will help you to pass the leaderless task.

TIP 1

Although you should not 'take over' the task, you should at every opportunity attempt to demonstrate leadership 'potential'. This can be achieved in a number of ways. Once the brief has been provided, be the first to speak out:

"OK everyone, shall we all form a plan in order to achieve the task in the most effective way possible? Does anyone have any suggestions as to how we can tackle this?"

TIP 2

I recommend that you use the words 'plan' and 'time' during the leaderless task and the command task. These two components are the cornerstone of effective teamwork.

TIP 3

Be supportive of other team members and shout words of encouragement:

"This is great team work everyone, keep going!"

<u>TIP 4</u>

If the facility exists, keep an eye on the time.

<u>TIP 5</u>

Suggest allocating tasks to people who have skills in certain areas. For example, if there are any knots that need to be tied, ask if there's anyone in the team who is competent in this area.

<u>TIP 6</u>

Keep going, even if things start to go wrong and time is running out. Remember to always act with a sense of urgency!

<u>TIP 7</u>

Be active and get involved.

The Command Task

The command task is different to the leaderless task in the fact that everyone in the group is required to take charge of an exercise/task.

You will be provided with a brief and you will then have a short period of time to brief the rest of your team and complete the required task. As you can imagine, the command task is harder than the leaderless task, simply because the spotlight is on you. It is crucial that you listen to the brief that will be provided by the boarding officer. Once you have the brief, you will then need to explain your plan to the rest of the group, allocate tasks and generally co-ordinate proceedings.

Briefing the Team

Once you have received the brief from the boarding officer you will have a short period of time to come up with a plan in order to achieve the task. Here is an excellent format to follow when briefing any team in a command situation:SMEAC

SITUATION

explain what the situation is.

"OK, gather around team and pay attention whilst I explain the situation. Our task today is to…"

MISSION

once you have explained the situation, tell the team what the mission is.

"Our mission is to…"

EXECUTION

tell your team how you are going to achieve the task including the allocation of tasks (plan).

"We will achieve the task by carrying out XYZ."

ASKING QUESTIONS

ask your team if anyone has any questions.

"Is the brief clear team? Does anyone have any questions?"

CHECK FOR UNDERSTANDING

check to see that your team fully understands what is expected from them.

"Is everyone clear of the team task and their role within the team?"

I have used SMEAC many times in the past during training exercises and also during firefighting operations. It provides a degree of organisation to any team and I would recommend that you learn it and use it during the command task when you are the person in charge.

Here's a list of tips to help you score higher during the command task exercise.

TIP 1

When you are not the person in charge, be an effective team member. Help out as much as possible and get stuck in! You may also wish to shout words of encouragement to the other members of the team.

"Let's keep going everyone, were doing a great job here."

TIP 2

When you are the allocated person in charge, take control of your team.

"OK everyone, gather around and pay attention to the following brief..."

TIP 3

Be supportive of your team members and get involved when necessary.

TIP 4

When briefing the team, consider using SMEAC.

TIP 5

If things start to go wrong, do not panic. Remain clam and in control. Keep going until the end and try your absolute hardest to complete the task. At the end of the task, whether it has been successful or not, thank your team for their efforts.

TIP 6

Keep an eye on safety. You are the person in charge and therefore responsible for safety.

CHAPTER 8
HOW TO PASS
THE OASC INTERVIEW

During this section of the guide I will provide you with a number of sample interview questions and advice on how to answer them. Whilst some of the questions will appear to be easy to answer, it is still important that we cover them, in order to ensure that you are fully prepared for your OASC.

I have divided the sample questions into various different sections to assist you during your preparation.

Section 1 - Personal questions

Q. When and where were you born?

Q. Where are you living now and who are you living with?

Q. Where else have you lived apart from with your parents?

Q. Describe your home life to me.

Q. What was your life like growing up?

Questions that relate to your home life are designed to assess how stable you are as a person, whether or not you have any responsibilities at home, whether you are generally a happy person and also what you have learnt from life's experiences to date.

• Know key dates of where you have lived;

• Try and provide examples of where you have moved around. This demonstrates that you are flexible and adaptable when the need arises;

• It is preferable that your home life is stable;

• The more responsibilities you have at home, such as washing, ironing, cleaning, financial responsibilities etc, the better;

• If you have lived with other people, apart from your immediate family, tell them so. Remember – as an RAF Officer you will be living with men and women of different ages etc.

Education

Q. How many schools have you attended and what years did you attend them?

Q. What did you think about your teachers?

Q. Tell me about your exam results; did you achieve the grades you wanted?

Q. Could you have worked harder whilst at school?

Although these are relatively easy questions to respond to, ones that relate to your exam results and how hard you worked whilst at school could catch you out. You have to be honest about your results. If they were not up to the standard that you expected, have a valid reason why. Never be disrespectful of your teachers or the educational system. Remember that you are applying to join a disciplined service.

School/College

Q. Did you learn anything from other students?

Q. Did you have any responsibilities whilst at school or college?

Q. What sports did you participate in whilst at school or college?

Q. What clubs or societies were you a member of?

Q. Do you have the Duke of Edinburgh or similar awards?

Q. Where did you travel with school?

Q. Did you have any gaps in your education?

If you did have any gaps in your education, it is better to say that you used the time wisely. Maybe you went travelling around the world in order to gain new experiences and cultures, or maybe you wanted to take time out from your studies to take on a work related role or even a charity role. Whatever you do, do not say that you did nothing with your time off. If you went travelling, what did you gain from the experience?

Whilst at school or college it would be an advantage if you had some level of responsibility. For example, maybe you were a prefect or head of year, or maybe you were the captain of a sports team. You are applying to become an Officer, which effectively means you are going to be a manager and a leader. Having some previous experience of these important roles will be an advantage. If you haven't had any responsibilities in your life to date, how do you know that you'll be a good leader or manager in the Air Force?

Outside Interests and Hobbies

Q. What sports are you currently engaged in?

Q. What sporting achievements have you gained?

Q. Have you been part of any youth organisations such as the Scouts or Guides?

Q. Describe your hobbies and interests.

Q. Are you currently employed either full-time or part-time?

Q. What did you do during your school holidays?

Q. Have you ever travelled? If so, where and when did you go and what did you gain from the experience(s)?

Q. What are you future ambitions or plans?

It is imperative that you demonstrate during the interview that you are an active person. If you sit at home all evening on your computer, playing games and surfing the net, then you are probably not the type of person the RAF are looking for. Demonstrate to the interviewer that you are active, a team player and have hobbies and interests that challenge you both mentally and physically.

Employment

Q. What jobs have you had to date?

Q. What responsibilities did you have during each job?

Q. Why did you leave each job?

Q. Did you complete any courses or gain any qualifications during each job?

Q. Who did you have to communicate with in each job?

Q. Were you part of a team or did you work alone?

Q. What were your appraisals like?

If you have no experience in a work related role to date, how do you know that you will be a good employee for the Royal Air Force? Make sure you have some work experience under your belt, even if it's part time work or charity work. Try to also provide examples of responsibilities during each work role and any managerial experience too. These will all work in your favour.

Motivational Questions

Q. Why do you want to join the RAF? Have you considered the Royal Navy or the Army?

Q. What specifically attracts you to the RAF?

Q. When did you first want to join and has anyone influenced you in your decision to join?

Q. Who have you talked to about a career in the RAF?

Q. How many visits have you had to the Armed Forces Careers Office?

Q. Have you previously attended OASC? If you have, what have you done to improve on last time?

Q. What contact have you had with the RAF? Have you visited any establishments or spoken to any serving members?

Q. Are there any disadvantages for you joining the RAF?

Q. What do your family and friends think of you joining?

Q. What branches of the RAF have you applied for?

Q. Would you consider any other branches of the RAF other than the one(s) you have chosen?

Q. What research have you carried out during your preparation for joining the Royal Air Force?

Q. Would you consider a Non-Commissioned role if you were unsuccessful at OASC?

Q. What length of commission/service would you like to work?

Q. What is role commission and what is SNCO?

Q. What qualities are required in order to become an RAF Officer?

Defend your branch choice as much as possible. In order to be capable of achieving this, you will need to know it inside out. Make sure you research key information about your chosen branch/career.

Knowledge of the Royal Air Force

Q. Tell me what you know about the history of the RAF.

Q. What training will you undergo as an Officer?

Q. Do you think you will have any problems or face any challenges during Initial Officer Training?

Q. Have you learnt anything about other branches of the Royal Air Force?

Q. Tell me what you know about the different aircrafts that serve in the RAF.

Q. How would you feel about going to war?

Q. Tell me about each of the different branches of the RAF.

Q. Where are the UK bases of the RAF?

Q. Whereabouts in the world are the RAF operating right now?

Q. What do you expect your secondary duties to be?

Q. Where and why would you expect to be based overseas?

Current Affairs Questions

Current affairs are a very important area of your preparation. You must carry out plenty of research in relation to current affairs. Not only will you need it during the interview(s), but it will also assist you during the group discussion.

Here are a few important tips to help you research current affairs effectively:

TIP 1

Be careful what paper(s) you read. The type of paper you read will reflect you as a person. If you tell the interviewer that you are an avid reader of The Sun or The Daily Star, you may not be Officer material. In the build up to OASC, try reading The Times, or another quality newspaper.

TIP 2

I would strongly recommend that you subscribe to The Week. This is a fantastic journal that will break down the week's stories for you. This will save having to buy lots of different newspapers.

You can subscribe to the week at the following website:
www.theweek.co.uk

TIP 3

Consider reading The Economist. Once again, this is a quality journal that will provide you with lots of current affairs information.

You can subscribe to The Economist at the following website:
www.economist.com

TIP 4

Don't just research affairs that are relevant to the RAF or the Armed Forces in general. Other topics are just as important!

The purpose of the current affairs section of the OASC interview is designed to assess how informed you are of current global affairs. You should have a general view on each subject and have an understanding of why the issue is important. Try to have a general view of the whole world with knowledge of a number of issues and events.

Use this format to help you research news and current affairs events:

• What is the subject?
• Why is it significant?
• What is your opinion on it?

Sample Current Affairs Questions

Q. Take me on a tour of the world and tell me what's caught your eye in the news recently.

Q. Tell me about 6 current affairs from abroad and six from home.

Q. Tell me about a news story from each continent.

Useful Websites

BBC News - www.bbc.co.uk/news/

The Times Online - www.timesonline.co.uk

NATO (North Atlantic Treaty Organisation) – www.nato.int

Ministry of Defence – www.mod.uk

Army – www.army.mod.uk

Royal Navy – www.royalnavy.mod.uk

Final Interview Tips

- Research key affairs from across the world.
- Have a broad knowledge of current affairs.
- Research affairs that have happened in the last 12 months.
- Focus in detail on events in the last 6 months.
- Select 6 topics for 'home' affairs (e.g. the budget, gang culture).
- Select 6 topics for 'away' affairs. Make sure that you use examples from right across the world.
- Gauge an opinion of each affair (you will need to be able to argue your point).
- Know key facts: people, numbers, locations etc.
- A firm handshake demonstrates a lot about your character.
- Be to the point and concise (don't waffle).
- Hold even eye contact with each boarding officer.
- Avoid hesitations such as "erm, ah, umm etc".
- Don't use slang.
- Sit up straight and don't slouch.
- Be confident but not overly so!
- Learn the dates and events listed on your application form.
- Make yourself stand out - do something different.
- Be aware of your weaknesses.
- Identify your strengths.
- Think before you speak.

Websites

THE ROYAL AIR FORCE (RAF) AND ASSOCIATED ORGANIZATIONS

The RAF	rafcareers.com
	raf.mod.uk
	rafrecruitment.co.uk
	rafweb.org
RAF Association	rafa.org.uk
RAF College Cranwell	cranwell.raf.mod.uk
Air Training Corps (ATC)	aircadets.org
Ministry of Defence	mod.uk

GENERAL CAREERS ADVICE

Learn Direct	learndirect-advice.co.uk
Courses & Careers in the UK	ca.courses-careers.com
Careers in Scotland	myworldofwork.co.uk
National Database of Accredited Qualifications	accreditedqualifications.org.uk
Prospects	prospects.ac.uk
Careers Advice	careers-guide.com

A FEW
FINAL WORDS

You have now reached the end of the guide and no doubt you will be ready to start preparing for the RAF Officer selection process. Just before you go off and start on your preparation, consider the following.

The majority of candidates who pass the RAF Officer selection process have a number of common factors. These are as follows:

1. They believe in themselves.

The first factor is self-belief. Regardless of what anyone tells you, you can pass the selection process and you can achieve high scores. Just like any job of this nature, you have to be prepared to work hard in order to be successful. The biggest piece of advice I can give to you is to concentrate on matching the assessable qualities that form part of the scoring criteria. These would be at the forefront of my mind if I was going through selection right now. Make sure you have the self-belief to pass the selection process and fill your mind with positive thoughts.

2. They prepare fully.

The second factor is preparation. Those people who achieve in life prepare fully for every eventuality and that is what you must do when you apply to become an Officer with the RAF. Work very hard and especially concentrate on your weak areas. Within this guide I have spoken a lot about preparation. Identify the areas that you are weak on and go all out to improve them.

3. They persevere.

Perseverance is a fantastic word. Everybody comes across obstacles or setbacks in their life, but it is what you do about those setbacks that is important. If you fail at something, then ask yourself 'why' have you failed? This will allow you to improve for next time and if you keep improving and trying, success will eventually follow. Apply this same method of thinking when you apply to join the RAF as an Officer.

4. They are self-motivated.

How much do you want to join the RAF? Do you want it, or do you *really* want it? When you apply to join the RAF you should want it more than anything in the world. Your levels of self motivation will shine through when you walk into the AFCO and when you attend the OASC. For the weeks and months leading up to the selection process, be motivated as best you can and always keep your fitness levels up as this will serve to increase your levels of motivation.

Work hard, stay focused and be what you want...

Richard McMunn

Richard McMunn

P.S. Come and spend a day with my team on our one day intensive RAF Officer OASC preparation course at the following website:

WWW.RAFOFFICERCOURSE.CO.UK

ATTEND OUR 1 DAY RAF OFFICER TRAINING COURSE

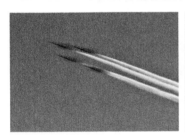

The people who are most likely to pass the Officer and Aircrew Selection Centre (OASC) are well-prepared and have an excellent understanding of how they are going to be assessed.

Whatever stage you are at in your application, or if you are yet to apply, our 1-day intensive Royal Air Force Officer Course will guide you and teach you exactly how to pass every element of the tough assessment process.

FOR MORE INFORMATION ON OUR RAF OFFICER TRAINING COURSE, PLEASE CHECK OUT THE FOLLOWING:

WWW.HOW2BECOME.COM

WANT MORE PRACTICE GUIDES TO HELP YOU PREPARE?

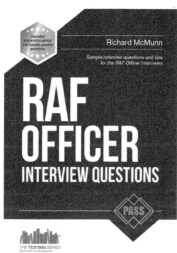

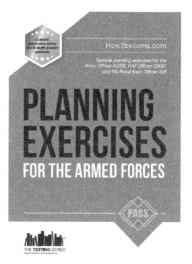

FOR MORE INFORMATION ON OUR ROYAL AIR FORCE GUIDES, PLEASE CHECK OUT THE FOLLOWING:

WWW.HOW2BECOME.COM

Get Access To

FREE

Psychometric Tests

www.PsychometricTestsOnline.co.uk

Printed in Great Britain
by Amazon